K3s Essentials

Definitive Reference for Developers and Engineers

Richard Johnson

Contents

Introduction

K3s represents a significant advancement in the landscape of container orchestration, offering a lightweight, efficient alternative to traditional Kubernetes distributions. Designed with simplicity and minimal resource consumption in mind, K3s addresses the growing demand for Kubernetes functionality in environments where conventional deployments may prove too resource-intensive or operationally complex. This book, *K3s Essentials*, is crafted to provide a comprehensive understanding of K3s, from its foundational concepts to advanced use cases, catering to practitioners who seek to deploy, manage, and optimize K3s clusters in diverse scenarios.

The evolution of lightweight Kubernetes solutions like K3s stems from the need to adapt container orchestration to edge computing, Internet of Things (IoT) networks, and other distributed systems with constrained resources. By streamlining the core components and integrating essential services into a remarkably compact binary, K3s offers agility without compromising the core capabilities of Kubernetes. Through this book, readers will explore the architectural nuances that differentiate K3s from upstream Kubernetes, gaining insight into the design considerations and trade-offs that enable its streamlined operation.

Installation and bootstrapping processes are critical for any orchestration platform, and K3s introduces unique approaches suited for rapid deployment and scaling, especially in resource-limited environments. This volume covers practical methods for establishing clusters, including high-availability configurations and support for various external datastores. Readers will also learn about automation techniques using popular tools, providing the operational foundation for managing K3s deployments effectively.

Understanding the internal architecture of K3s is paramount to mastering its capabilities and troubleshooting potential issues. The book delves into its component packaging, integrated add-ons, and the modifications applied to the Kubernetes API surface. Such detailed examination fosters a deeper comprehension of K3s's operational mechanisms, including node lifecycle management and storage backend options, equipping readers to tailor deployments to their specific requirements.

Networking plays a pivotal role in container orchestration, and K3s supports a range of network configurations from default overlay networks to sophisticated service meshes. This text explores supported container network interfaces, ingress controllers, load balancing techniques, and strategies for securing cluster communication. Comprehensive coverage of these subjects ensures that readers can design resilient, secure, and performant network architectures aligned with their infrastructure needs.

Storage and data management are integral to the reliability of applications running on K3s. The book addresses the management of ephemeral and persistent data, configuration of volumes and storage classes, implementation of the Container Storage Interface, and specialized patterns for edge and IoT use cases. Topics such as backup, disaster recovery, and secrets management are presented with attention to maintaining data integrity and compliance in production environments.

Security considerations permeate all aspects of deploying and operating Kubernetes, and K3s is no exception. This work provides guidance on cluster hardening, role-based access control, runtime protection, and supply chain security. Readers will find in-depth analysis of policy enforcement frameworks, multi-tenancy models, and audit strategies that support regulatory compliance and operational governance.

Observability and monitoring are essential to maintain performance and reliability. Detailed guidance on metrics collection, logging architectures, tracing, and autoscaling is included to empower operators with tools for proactive management. Special focus on remote monitoring addresses the complexities of managing edge and multi-cluster environments.

As K3s continues to mature, its role in scaling, multi-cluster orchestration, and lifecycle operations expands. Practical approaches to node management, rollouts, GitOps integration, and high-availability configurations are explored to assist organizations in achieving robust, scalable deployments.

Finally, advanced use cases and integration patterns demonstrate K3s's versatility beyond foundational applications, including deployment in edge and IoT ecosystems, support for AI and machine learning workloads, and extension with emerging technologies like WebAssembly. Considerations for hybrid cloud orchestration and legacy application modernization illustrate K3s's capacity to unify diverse operational domains.

This book aims to serve as a definitive resource for practitioners, architects, and engineers who seek to leverage K3s to its fullest potential. With an emphasis on clarity, rigor, and practical insights, *K3s Essentials* presents a structured, thorough examination of K3s that will support the effective design, deployment, and operation of lightweight Kubernetes environments in modern IT infrastructures.

Chapter 1

Foundations of K3s and Lightweight Kubernetes

Why did cloud native technology need something slimmer than Kubernetes? This chapter journeys through the motivations and vision behind K3s, revealing how its lightweight design fundamentally reimagines container orchestration for new frontiers like the edge, IoT, and resource-constrained deployments. As we build the historical and technical context, you'll discover not just how K3s differs, but why those differences matter for innovators and operators alike.

1.1. Origins and Motivation

The evolution of container orchestration systems has been marked by a growing need for scalable, reliable platforms capable of managing complex workloads in diverse environments. Kubernetes emerged as the de facto standard for container orchestration due to its robust feature set, extensibility, and large community support. However, its initial design was primarily focused on large-scale data centers and cloud infrastructures with ample computational resources. This orientation presented significant challenges when adapting Kubernetes to resource-constrained environments such as edge computing, Internet of Things (IoT) deployments, and embedded systems.

Traditional Kubernetes distributions are architected with components like the API server, controller manager, scheduler, kubelet, and etcd running several system processes, expecting high availability and persistent, reliable networking. These components, while essential to Kubernetes' robustness, impose considerable resource demands in terms of CPU, memory, and storage. The minimum memory footprint for running a standard Kubernetes cluster often exceeds hundreds of megabytes per node, which is prohibitive for devices with limited capacity. Moreover, the operational complexity, including dependency management and ongoing maintenance efforts, further complicates deployment in distributed, heterogeneous, and intermittently connected edge environments.

The latency-sensitive nature of edge workloads introduces additional constraints, as applications must often respond in milliseconds, rendering centralized control planes and heavy inter-node communication ineffective. The dynamic and sometimes unreliable network conditions characteristic of remote or embedded deployments necessitate an orchestration solution capable of functioning with intermittent connectivity and minimal coordination overhead. The security posture also requires reassessment, as devices at the network edge present diverse threat models that differ significantly from traditional cloud environments.

Recognizing these constraints, the industry sought lighter and more resource-efficient Kubernetes variants that preserve core orchestration capabilities while minimizing complexity and footprint. This need catalyzed the development of lightweight Kubernetes distributions, with K3s being a prominent example. Launched by Rancher Labs in 2019, K3s was explicitly designed to address the shortcomings of standard Kubernetes in constrained environments, streamlining operation without sacrificing compliance with the Kubernetes API and ecosystem.

K3s unifies the entire control plane and node components into a single binary, with an architecture optimized for low resource consumption. It replaces components such as etcd with embedded lightweight alternatives like SQLite by default, while optionally supporting external datastores for enhanced scalability. This architectural simplification reduces the dependencies, installation friction, and operational glitches typical of traditional Kubernetes setups. K3s also strips away certain alpha and non-essential features to maintain a lean, stable core, ensuring reliability without the weight of superfluous modules irrelevant to edge scenarios.

From an organizational and ecosystem perspective, K3s's development fits into a broader motivation to democratize Kubernetes for emerging use cases. The Cloud Native Computing Foundation (CNCF) recognized the importance of such projects by incorporating K3s into its Sandbox program, providing governance, visibility, and a collaborative framework for enhancement. This acceptance validated the strategic significance of lightweight distributions as a complement to mainstream Kubernetes deployments, fostering innovation in edge orchestration.

The vision behind K3s extends beyond mere reduction of resource requirements. It aims to enable real-world deployment scenarios such as industrial IoT systems, autonomous vehicles, remote monitoring stations, and small-scale on-premises clusters that demand resilient, consistent orchestration yet cannot sustain the overhead of full Kubernetes. K3s fosters portability, rapid iteration, and ease of integration, aligning with the principles of cloud-native computing adapted for diverse operational topologies.

Early iterations of K3s demonstrated the viability of container orchestration on constrained hardware such as ARM-based single-board computers and small VM instances. Its adaptability in heterogeneous environments—ranging from disconnected edge sites to intermittent GSM networks—highlighted the importance of modularity, optional components, and minimalism in cluster management. The project's rapid community adoption and contributions reflected a widespread recognition of its addressing a previously unmet need within the Kubernetes ecosystem.

In summary, the creation of lightweight Kubernetes distributions like K3s was motivated by the technological limitations of traditional Kubernetes in edge, IoT, and small-footprint environments, coupled with organizational initiatives to extend Kubernetes usability beyond large-scale cloud datacenters. By balancing full Kubernetes compatibility with substantial reduction in resource demands and complexity, projects such as K3s embody a strategic shift towards inclusive, adaptable orchestration platforms designed for the future's distributed and heterogeneous infrastructure landscape.

1.2. Core Architectural Differences with Kubernetes

K3s represents a deliberate reimagining of Kubernetes, tailored specifically to meet the needs of lightweight and resource-constrained environments without compromising core orchestration functionalities. This section elucidates the principal architectural divergences from upstream Kubernetes, focusing on binary size reduction, the excision of non-essential components, deployment simplification, and targeted optimizations for small architectures. Each design decision is analyzed in the context of its rationale and operational implications.

8

Binary Size Reduction

The upstream Kubernetes distribution maintains a comprehensive yet complex codebase designed for enterprise-scale deployments, which inevitably results in a large binary footprint. K3s addresses this issue by aggressively pruning the binary size. The primary mechanism involves statically compiling a single monolithic binary that bundles the Kubernetes control plane components. This contrasts with the upstream approach that deploys multiple loosely coupled binaries, such as `kube-apiserver`, `kube-controller-manager`, and `kube-scheduler`, each operating as independent processes.

By consolidating these components into one executable, K3s eliminates inter-process communication overhead and reduces image size significantly-by an order of magnitude compared to standard Kubernetes binaries. Additionally, K3s swaps out certain dependencies for lighter alternatives; for example, it utilizes an embedded SQLite datastore by default instead of etcd, which removes the need to run a separate distributed key-value store cluster. For users requiring high availability, K3s supports an optional external etcd or database backend.

From an operational perspective, this binary consolidation substantially simplifies deployment and updates, encourages minimal resource consumption, and lowers the barrier for edge and IoT use cases where system resources and bandwidth are scarce.

Removal of Non-Essential Components

K3s selectively omits or disables components deemed non-essential for typical lightweight or single-node environments. Crucial Kubernetes add-ons and controllers with minimal impact on small clusters-such as `PodSecurityPolicy`, core DNS components beyond a basic DNS server, and certain admission controllers-are either stripped out or replaced with simpler implementations.

One notable omission is the default removal of alpha and beta features that are unstable or uncommonly used, thus reducing complexity and potential bugs. In addition, cloud provider integrations and network plugins typical of upstream Kubernetes, which assume sophisticated cloud infrastructure, are not bundled by default. Instead, K3s provides a straightforward container network interface (CNI) option, `flannel`-based by default, optimized for simplicity and ease of configuration.

K3s also integrates a lightweight container runtime, `containerd`, embedded directly rather than relying on external Docker daemons, which improves startup times and reduces memory overhead. This runtime choice aligns with smaller footprints and less operational complexity.

These removals and substitutions improve runtime efficiency and stability, trimming the attack surface and operational noise while retaining the critical APIs and controllers required for cluster management, scheduling, and workload lifecycle.

Simplified Deployment Model

One of the hallmark architectural choices in K3s is the emphasis on ease of deployment, especially for decentralized and edge-node deployments where operations personnel may lack extensive Kubernetes expertise. K3s achieves this goal through several key characteristics:

- *Single binary deployment*: As noted, the monolithic binary simplifies installation procedures.

- *Minimal configuration requirements*: Default configurations are sensible and self-contained, obviating the need for complex manifests or external dependencies for most scenarios.

- *Automated certificate management*: K3s automates TLS key and certificate generation, renewal, and distribution across nodes, eliminating typically error-prone manual steps.

- *Embedded service components*: Components such as the service proxy (via an embedded `klipper-lb`) replace more complex load balancers, reducing the requirement for separate infrastructure.

These aspects manifest operational benefits by markedly reducing time-to-first-cluster and facilitating rapid prototyping or production deployment on constrained hardware with minimal manual intervention.

Optimizations for Small Architectures

K3s's design accommodates a spectrum of hardware architectures, including ARM32 and ARM64 processors, which are common in edge devices and embedded systems. This support entails cross-compilation and architecture-specific optimizations to maintain performance and compatibility.

Resource usage optimizations permeate the K3s architecture, manifested as:

- *Lower memory consumption*: Memory footprint is minimized by disabling unnecessary features, using lightweight storage backends, and employing minimal dependencies.

- *Reduced CPU overhead*: Tight coupling of control plane components and the use of native Go libraries with optimized resource management reduces CPU churn.

- *Storage layer simplification*: The default SQLite datastore avoids the overhead of distributed storage replication while providing sufficient durability for single-node scenarios.

- *Small image sizes*: Container images are optimized for minimum size, which accelerates pulls and reduces disk usage.

Operationally, these optimizations enable K3s to run smoothly on devices with as little as 512 MB RAM and single-core CPUs, broadening Kubernetes applicability beyond traditional data center environments without sacrificing orchestration fidelity.

Operational Impacts of Architectural Choices

While K3s delivers notable advantages through its tailored architectural decisions, it also introduces trade-offs that system architects must consider.

The reliance on SQLite as a default datastore restricts scale and multi-node high availability, though clustering options and external databases are supported for production-grade environments. The omission of certain upstream features, while simplifying operational overhead, may limit the capability set for workloads requiring specific Kubernetes extensions or policies.

The monolithic binary architecture, although beneficial for deployment and resource usage, could complicate debugging and component replacement, as all functions are encapsulated in one executable. Additionally, K3s's lightweight service load balancer is appropriate for edge or small-scale deployments but may necessitate integration with external load balancers for production load distribution.

In sum, the architectural deviations that define K3s are strategic compromises aimed at maximizing lightweight operation, deployment ease, and edge readiness. For scenarios aligning with these parameters, K3s delivers a robust, compliant Kubernetes experience with operational simplicity unattainable by upstream Kubernetes defaults.

In accordance with its design ethos, K3s continually evolves, selectively integrating upstream improvements while maintaining its core goal of preserving a minimalist, efficient Kubernetes distribution optimized for small footprints and operational simplicity.

1.3. Supported Platforms and System Requirements

K3s is designed to be a lightweight Kubernetes distribution optimized for resource-constrained environments while retaining compatibility with standard Kubernetes APIs and tools. Its support for diverse platforms and architectures is a core factor contributing to its widespread adoption, particularly in edge computing, IoT deployments, and development workflows involving heterogeneous hardware.

Operating Systems

K3s officially supports a broad range of operating systems, with a primary focus on Linux distributions. The supported Linux OS variants include, but are not limited to:

- **Ubuntu:** Versions 18.04 and later are reliably supported, leveraging Ubuntu's LTS stability.

- **Debian:** Debian 10 (Buster) and subsequent releases provide a stable base for K3s installations.

- **CentOS and Rocky Linux:** Both CentOS 7/8 and compatible RHEL derivatives serve as supported platforms, given their widespread enterprise adoption.

- **Alpine Linux:** Due to its minimalist design, Alpine is frequently used in containerized environments and supports K3s, although with some caveats around glibc versus musl compatibility.

While Linux remains the predominant supported OS family, K3s has experimental support in specific configurations for Windows nodes. The Windows nodes act as worker nodes within a K3s cluster but require a Linux-based control plane. Such hybrid clusters allow leveraging Windows-specific workloads while maintaining

Kubernetes orchestration. However, this capability is evolving and may necessitate careful alignment of Windows Server versions and container runtime compatibility.

Hardware Architectures

K3s distinguishes itself by supporting multiple CPU architectures, significantly broadening its applicability in embedded, ARM-based devices, and standard x86 environments. The two principal hardware architectures officially supported include:

- x86_64 (amd64): The dominant architecture for server-class hardware, desktops, and cloud VMs. K3s fully supports this architecture with optimized binaries and container images.

- ARM (armhf and arm64): Support extends to both 32-bit ARM hard-float (armhf) and 64-bit ARM (arm64) architectures. This enables deployment on Raspberry Pi series devices, ARM-based servers such as AWS Graviton processors, NVIDIA Jetson, and other ARM-powered edge devices.

This cross-architecture support is facilitated by multi-architecture container images and statically compiled K3s binaries. As a result, K3s can function on devices ranging from resource-limited single-board computers to industrial-grade ARM servers, enabling sophisticated Kubernetes automation in novel hardware contexts.

Virtualization and Container Environments

Virtualized environments form a critical segment of the supported platform ecosystem. K3s functions effectively on standard hypervisor-based virtual machines, including but not limited to:

- **VMware ESXi:** Common in enterprise data centers, K3s clusters can be deployed on virtual machines provisioned within ESXi environments.

- **KVM/QEMU:** Open-source virtualization platforms widely used for local development and cloud infrastructure.

- **Microsoft Hyper-V:** Support for Windows-based hypervisors extends K3s clusters into mixed OS virtualization scenarios.

- **Cloud environments:** Public clouds such as AWS, Google Cloud, and Azure provide virtualized infrastructure where K3s can be installed directly or as part of managed Kubernetes offerings.

Regarding container runtimes, K3s includes a lightweight container engine, containerd, by default. This choice reduces overhead in virtualized and bare-metal environments. Additionally, K3s's internal components are packaged to work out-of-the-box with the included containerd, though alternative container runtimes may be integrated with appropriate configuration changes.

Minimum and Recommended System Requirements

Understanding minimum and recommended hardware requirements is vital for effective K3s deployment, especially in heterogeneous environments where resources are constrained or unconventional.

Control Plane Requirements:

The control plane node(s) manage the Kubernetes API server, scheduler, controller manager, and the embedded SQLite or external datastore persistence layer.

- *Minimum:* A single node with at least 512 MiB of RAM and 1 CPU core can run K3s control plane functions for minimal, non-production workloads and testing.

- *Recommended:* For production-grade clusters, at least 2 GiB of RAM and 2 CPU cores are advised to accommodate critical control plane components, API responsiveness, and control loop processing.

Worker Node Requirements:

Worker nodes run application workloads, and their requirements vary significantly depending on container resource demands.

- *Minimum:* 512 MiB RAM and a single CPU core can be sufficient for simple workload containers, small IoT tasks, or constrained edge nodes.

- *Recommended:* 1–2 GiB RAM and multiple CPU cores per worker node offer performance headroom for multi-container pods and moderate traffic.

Storage Considerations:

K3s supports ephemeral and persistent storage backends. For embedded and single-node clusters, an embedded SQLite database is the default backend, which requires significantly less resource overhead compared to etcd but limits scalability. Production clusters generally rely on external etcd or cloud-backed storage solutions.

Versatility in Unique Hardware Scenarios

K3s's architecture emphasizes portability and minimal dependencies. This is evidenced in deployments on unique and diverse hardware scenarios such as:

- **Raspberry Pi Clusters:** Multi-node ARMv8 (arm64) Raspberry Pi 4 clusters running K3s have become a canonical example of K3s's ability to deliver mainstream Kubernetes functionality in an under-4-GB RAM environment.

- **Industrial IoT Gateways:** Devices running custom Linux kernels on ARM Cortex-A family chips, often with constrained I/O and flash storage, rely on K3s to orchestrate containerized analytics and edge automation workloads.

- **ARM-based Cloud Instances:** Cloud providers offering ARM instances (e.g., AWS Graviton2) benefit from K3s's native arm64 support to optimize costs and power efficiency without sacrificing Kubernetes compatibility.

- **Mixed-Architecture Clusters:** K3s supports hybrid environments where control plane nodes run on x86_64 servers and worker nodes run ARM devices or vice versa, provided container images support multi-architecture manifests.

This hardware versatility is accompanied by K3s's lightweight design choices, such as removing legacy alpha features in Kubernetes, integrating with embedded SQLite by default, and tightly coupling with containerd, all of which minimize resource footprints and enhance compatibility across diverse platforms.

Category	Description/Examples
Operating Systems	Ubuntu, Debian, CentOS/Rocky, Alpine Linux, experimental Windows worker nodes
Hardware Architectures	x86_64 (amd64), ARMv7/armhf (32-bit), ARM64 (aarch64)
Virtualization	VMware ESXi, KVM/QEMU, Hyper-V, public clouds (AWS, Azure, Google Cloud)
Minimum System Specs	Control Plane: 512 MiB RAM, 1 CPU core; Worker: 512 MiB RAM, 1 CPU core
Recommended Specs	Control Plane: 2 GiB RAM, 2+ CPU cores; Worker: 1–2 GiB RAM, multiple CPU cores
Unique Hardware Cases	Raspberry Pi clusters, ARM cloud instances, industrial IoT gateways, hybrid clusters

By accommodating such a wide variety of environments, K3s provides a flexible and efficient Kubernetes distribution suited for the full spectrum of modern cloud-native and edge use cases. The adaptability to heterogeneous hardware settings and modest resource requirements fundamentally expands the operational envelope of Kubernetes orchestrations.

1.4. Use Cases and Deployment Scenarios

K3s stands out as an optimized, lightweight Kubernetes distribution designed specifically for resource-constrained environments and streamlined orchestration needs. Its flexibility and minimal resource footprint enable a diverse range of deployment scenarios, addressing challenges from edge computing to cloud-native development infrastructures.

A primary domain where K3s excels is at the network edge, a paradigm shift driven by latency-sensitive applications, bandwidth constraints, and localized data processing requirements. Edge deployments often involve numerous geographically dispersed nodes with limited computational and power resources, such as gateways, industrial controllers, or micro data centers. K3s fits this model by requiring significantly fewer CPU and memory resources than standard Kubernetes, eliminating the need for extensive control plane components while retaining full Kubernetes API compatibility. For example, deploying K3s on ARM-based SoCs used in IoT gateways allows real-time processing of sensor data, anomaly detection, and local decision-making without continuous cloud reliance. This reduces network load and latency, improving responsiveness in scenarios like smart manufacturing, autonomous vehicle coordination, or remote healthcare monitoring.

IoT device orchestration also benefits from K3s's minimalist design. Many IoT use cases demand lightweight, resilient orchestration on heterogeneous hardware environments. K3s supports edge device clusters where containerized applications perform tasks including telemetry collection, local AI inference, or protocol translation. Its simplified architecture enables automatic node registration, built-in containerd runtime, and a small binary footprint conducive to frequent OTA updates. These capabilities facilitate seamless fleet management and decentralized application upgrades in contexts such as smart agriculture, energy grid management, or retail analytics kiosks.

Within continuous integration and continuous delivery (CI/CD) pipelines, K3s serves as an efficient testbed and runtime environment. Conventional Kubernetes installations often necessitate extensive resource allocation and setup overhead, limiting the ability to run ephemeral clusters dynamically during automated builds or integration tests. K3s, with its rapid startup time and minimal dependencies, can be provisioned in ephemeral virtual machines or containers, providing realistic Kubernetes environments for testing application manifests, Helm charts, and operator behaviors. Development teams leverage K3s to mimic production cluster behavior without incurring the cost of full-scale clusters. Its compatibility with standard Kubernetes tools ensures that CI/CD workflows transfer seamlessly between local pipelines and cloud preferences, enhancing developer productivity and reducing pipeline complexity.

K3s is also widely adopted as a development testbed for proof-of-concept (PoC) and multi-cluster experimentation. Developers needing to evaluate microservices architectures, service meshes, or custom controllers benefit from K3s's low-friction installation on laptops, desktops, or private lab hardware. It supports multi-node cluster configurations on minimal infrastructure, enabling the study of advanced Kubernetes features such as network policies, load balancing, and persistent storage integration. For instance, software teams can rapidly iterate on Kubernetes-native applications by deploying them on K3s clusters hosted within lightweight virtualized or containerized environments, minimizing context switches and infrastructure costs.

Hybrid cloud scenarios expand K3s's applicability by bridging on-premises, public cloud, and edge environments under a cohesive Kubernetes control plane strategy. Enterprises increasingly demand infrastructure agility that permits workload migration or bursting across multiple physical locations without rewriting orchestration logic. K3s's small footprint facilitates deployment on edge sites or private data centers, while its upstream Kubernetes compatibility ensures that configuration, security, and observability tools remain consistent. This approach streamlines development and operations workflows, enabling applications to scale dynamically between clouds and edge with unified policy enforcement. Real-world deployments include retail chains running K3s on edge servers within stores coupled with cloud-based central management, or telecommunications operators deploying micro clusters for 5G mobile edge compute (MEC) scenarios.

Typical deployment patterns exploiting K3s's strengths include:

- **Single-node edge clusters**: Ideal for localized services requiring near-instant deployment and low maintenance overhead, such as gateway proxies or local data aggregation agents.

- **Multi-node lightweight edge clusters**: Deployed across constrained hardware with minimal redundancy for high availability and load distribution, supporting critical real-time processing workloads.

- **Ephemeral CI/CD clusters**: Dynamically created and destroyed within pipeline agents or build farms to conduct isolated Kubernetes integration tests.

- **Hybrid edge-cloud clusters**: Interlinked K3s clusters managed via federated control planes or GitOps workflows, facilitating workload portability and consistent policy enforcement.

- **Development sandboxes**: Developer- or QA-managed K3s clusters on workstations or internal servers for prototyping and early validation.

In practice, these scenarios leverage K3s's bundled components-such as embedded SQLite or lightweight database options for cluster state, and integrated service load balancers-to reduce external dependencies. Moreover, the default container runtime, containerd, harmonizes the container lifecycle closer to minimalism and stability, decreasing the attack surface and simplifying maintenance.

Operational case studies illustrate real-world benefits. At a smart city deployment, K3s clusters operate on street-level kiosks to perform localized data preprocessing from environmental sensors, reducing bandwidth costs and enabling rapid response to air quality anomalies. A global retail enterprise adopted K3s to manage their IoT device fleet firmware updates through containerized rolling deployments, achieving near-zero downtime and simplified rollback capabilities. Software companies utilize K3s as part of their developer cloud infrastructure to simulate multi-cluster topologies and validate emerging Kubernetes operators and custom resource definitions in realistic yet resource-efficient environments.

The intrinsic versatility and streamlined architecture of K3s render it an enabling technology for scenarios where traditional Kubernetes distributions would be prohibitive due to size, complexity, or resource consumption. Its alignment with edge-first design principles, combined with full Kubernetes ecosystem compatibility, ensures that K3s is uniquely positioned to meet evolving demands spanning edge computing, IoT management, continuous integration workflows, developer environments, and hybrid cloud orchestration.

1.5. Project Governance and Ecosystem

K3s operates under a governance model typical of successful open source projects, blending structured roles with community-driven collaboration to ensure sustainable development, transparency, and innovation. The governance structure establishes clear responsibilities for maintainers while actively encouraging contributions from a diverse range of participants, including individual developers, enterprises, and end-users.

At the core, K3s governance is overseen by a group of maintainers who hold the authority to review, approve, and merge changes to the codebase. These maintainers are selected based on sustained contributions and demonstrated expertise in both Kubernetes concepts and the particularities of K3s. They ensure that all modifications adhere to coding standards, performance benchmarks, and security best practices. Maintainers also serve as stewards of the project's strategic direction, balancing feature requests, bug fixes, and long-term enhancements.

Contributors span a wider community and constitute the lifeblood of the project. Their responsibilities range from submitting patches and reporting issues to creating documentation and engaging in discussions on design decisions. Contributors typically propose changes via pull requests, which undergo rigorous peer review to maintain quality and coherence. This peer-review process frequently involves automated testing through continuous integration pipelines, guaranteeing stability across diverse platforms supported by K3s.

The development lifecycle follows a cadence aligned with upstream Kubernetes releases but is adapted to K3s's goals around lightness and ease of use. Feature development prioritizes simplicity and minimal resource consumption without sacrificing compatibility. Releases are categorized into stable, release candidate, and experimental branches, fostering an environment where new ideas can be trialed safely before general adoption. Release managers, often maintainers themselves, coordinate version cutoffs, documentation updates, and community notification.

Beyond the core project, K3s has cultivated a rich ecosystem of integrations, extensions, and community-driven projects that amplify its functionality and adoption in various environments. This ecosystem includes components such as lightweight ingress controllers, container runtimes optimized for edge devices, and customized storage plugins tailored to embedded systems. Many of these are officially recognized or endorsed by the maintainers, further linking them into the project's quality assurance framework.

Several community projects have emerged to address the needs of specific deployment scenarios. For instance, specialized operator frameworks facilitate the deployment of K3s clusters on Internet of Things (IoT) gateways, enabling container orchestration in environments with intermittent connectivity and constrained hardware. Extensions also exist for enhanced security features, integrating with service meshes and policy enforcement tools designed for minimal overhead.

Integration with cloud-native tools spans monitoring, logging, and observability platforms that support lightweight deployment models. Frameworks such as Prometheus exporters tailored for edge workloads and adaptive logging systems that handle ephemeral data streams exemplify the ecosystem's breadth. This interoperability ensures K3s can fit seamlessly into existing DevOps pipelines and management platforms, thereby lowering adoption barriers.

The community's active engagement is fostered through mailing lists, dedicated forums, regular virtual meetings, and documentation sprints. These venues facilitate knowledge sharing, roadmap discussions, and collaborative problem-solving. Moreover, governance transparency is maintained by publicly accessible issue trackers and decision logs, allowing contributors and users to track project evolution and participate in shaping its future.

Commercial entities that rely on K3s often contribute back by sponsoring features or resources, providing security audits, and supporting the documentation ecosystem. Such symbiotic relationships reinforce K3s's position as both an open project and a foundational technology for production-grade deployments, especially in edge and resource-constrained environments.

In sum, the governance and ecosystem surrounding K3s exemplify a balance between disciplined stewardship and vibrant community participation. This balance enables rapid innovation while ensuring reliability and alignment with Kubernetes standards. As a result, K3s continues to expand its footprint within the container orchestration landscape, buoyed by a thriving network of collaborators and a growing collection of integrative technologies.

1.6. Security Posture and Threat Landscape

K3s is engineered as a lightweight Kubernetes distribution optimized for resource-constrained environments. While its minimalistic design enhances deployment agility and operational simplicity, it also necessitates a nuanced understanding of its security posture and the associated threat landscape. This section elucidates essential security considerations intrinsic to K3s, focusing on its default security model, potential exposure vectors introduced by its streamlined architecture, and recommended mitigations for production deployments.

The default security model of K3s retains core Kubernetes security principles but applies pragmatic adjustments to its resource footprint. For example, K3s consolidates several control plane components, such as the API server, scheduler, and controller manager, into a single binary, reducing inter-component communication complexity and resource overhead. This architectural choice inherently minimizes the attack surface by limiting network bindings and simplifying authentication pathways. Additionally, K3s employs the embedded SQLite datastore by default for single-node clusters, eliminating the need for external etcd dependencies and their corresponding exposure. However, in multi-node or high-availability configurations, K3s supports external datastores such as MySQL, Postgres, and etcd, where the security of datastore credentials, network segmentation, and encryption becomes critical.

Despite the streamlined design, several exposure points deserve emphasis. First, the minimal default installation disables certain Kubernetes features that carry inherent risks but also removes components commonly leveraged for robust security controls, such as Pod Security Policies (PSPs), now deprecated. As K3s bypasses PSPs, operators must consider alternative mechanisms like Open Policy Agent (OPA) Gatekeeper or Kyverno to enforce pod-level security constraints. Moreover, K3s enables container runtime interface (CRI) features via containerd, which inherits its own attack surface and privilege escalation risks if not properly confined and updated.

Another significant exposure arises from network configuration and ingress handling. K3s utilizes a simplified networking stack, commonly integrating lightweight CNI plugins such as Flannel or Calico in its default mode. While these plugins enable connectivity, their default configurations may allow broader communication than intended if network policies are not explicitly defined and enforced. Furthermore, default service accounts and role-based access control (RBAC) settings require meticulous review to avoid privilege sprawl, as Kubernetes' complexity can inadvertently grant cluster-wide permissions. K3s, by embedding a default service account and simplified token management, mandates explicit RBAC hardening aligned with the principle of least privilege.

The architecture of K3s incorporates several mechanisms that address common Kubernetes threats. Mutual Transport Layer Security (mTLS) is enabled by default for cluster component communication, reducing the risk of man-in-the-middle attacks during API interactions. Furthermore, K3s automates the generation and lifecycle management of TLS certificates for the API server, Kubelet, and other cluster components, mitigating risks associated with manual certificate handling errors. In addition, the inclusion of a built-in Helm controller facilitates secure application deployment with integrated signature verification and proper namespace scoping.

Mitigation strategies for production environments emphasize layering security controls beyond default K3s safeguards. Network segmentation through granular network policies is imperative-restricting pod-to-pod and pod-to-external communications to explicit pathways. Enforcing admission control policies using OPA Gatekeeper or Kyverno supplements the limited default security policies, implementing controls over resource creation, pod security contexts, and sensitive configuration settings. Enabling and monitoring audit logging within K3s offers transparency into cluster activity, facilitating early detection of anomalous behavior or unauthorized access attempts.

Credential management deserves particular attention. Operators must securely provision, rotate, and restrict access to service account tokens, kubeconfig files, and datastore credentials. Integrating secrets management systems such as HashiCorp Vault or Kubernetes External Secrets enhances the protection of sensitive information beyond Kubernetes' native secrets, which are base64 encoded but not encrypted by default. Moreover, K3s supports Trusted Platform Module (TPM) attestation and secure boot mechanisms on compatible hardware, hardening the underlying host environment against firmware and boot-level attacks.

Container security best practices complement these measures, including the use of minimal and vetted container images, enabling read-only root filesystems, and configuring Linux security modules (e.g., SELinux, AppArmor) appropriately within K3s nodes to prevent privilege escalation. Regular patching of the K3s binaries, container runtimes, and operating system components is crucial to remediate vulnerabilities disclosed through continuous vulnerability assessments and threat intelligence.

Finally, the security posture of a K3s cluster is strongly influenced by the operator's environment and operational discipline. Proper isolation of management interfaces, use of VPNs or private networks, and limiting administrative access via multi-factor authentication and just-in-time access controls are essential components in reducing the attack surface. Backup and disaster recovery plans incorporating encrypted snapshots of cluster states and consistent testing of restore procedures ensure resilience against data corruption or ransomware incidents.

K3s presents a secure foundation compatible with diverse operational scenarios, but its minimalist paradigm imposes a demand for comprehensive, multi-layered security strategies. By understanding the underlying architectural decisions, exposure points, and security controls, operators can deploy K3s clusters with confidence, balancing simplicity and robustness within evolving threat landscapes.

Chapter 2

Installation and Bootstrapping of K3s Clusters

Launching a Kubernetes cluster shouldn't be rocket science. This chapter demystifies the process with practical, step-by-step strategies to get K3s up and running—no matter your scale, platform, or resource limits. From one-liner quickstarts to robust, automated fleets, discover how easy yet powerful K3s deployment can be.

2.1. Quickstart: From Zero to Cluster

A minimal K3s cluster can be launched rapidly, providing a lightweight, production-grade Kubernetes environment suitable for development, IoT, edge, and CI workloads. This quickstart details the most common installation methods, focusing on the canonical install script, and highlights key troubleshooting tips to ensure cluster readiness in minutes.

K3s is distributed as a single binary, minimizing prerequisites for setting up a Kubernetes cluster. The simplest method to deploy a single-node cluster is through the official install script, which automates the download and configuration processes. This approach is highly recommended for both first-time users and advanced practitioners seeking immediate results.

Single-Node Cluster Installation via Script

The canonical command invocation is:

```
curl -sfL https://get.k3s.io | sh -
```

This command fetches the install script and pipes it directly to a shell interpreter with default options. Specifically, it installs K3s as a systemd service, manages dependencies, and initiates the cluster with a single node acting as both the server and agent.

Upon successful completion, the script saves configuration details and credentials in the directory /etc/rancher/k3s. The kubectl client configuration file is available at /etc/rancher/k3s/k3s.yaml, which can be copied to $HOME/.kube/config for standard Kubernetes CLI usage.

Verify cluster status with:

```
sudo k3s kubectl get nodes
```

Expected output should show a single node with the Ready status:

```
NAME              STATUS   ROLES                  AGE   VERSION
hostname.local    Ready    control-plane,master   1m    v1.26.3+k3s1
```

The install script supports optional environment variables to adjust behavior such as choosing a specific Kubernetes version or customizing data storage locations. For example, to install K3s version v1.26.3+k3s1 explicitly:

```
curl -sfL https://get.k3s.io | INSTALL_K3S_VERSION=v1.26.3+k3s1
    sh -
```

Multi-Node Clusters: Server and Agent Roles

K3s employs a lightweight architecture with one or more *servers* coordinating the cluster and *agents* executing workloads. After preparing the primary server node as above, additional nodes can be added as agents.

Begin by extracting the K3s server node token, essential for agent authentication:

```
sudo cat /var/lib/rancher/k3s/server/node-token
```

On each candidate agent node, run:

```
curl -sfL https://get.k3s.io | K3S_URL=https://<server-ip>:6443 \
    K3S_TOKEN=<node-token> sh -
```

Replace `<server-ip>` with the IP address or DNS name of the server node and `<node-token>` with the token obtained above. This operation installs and launches the K3s agent service, connecting it to the cluster.

Confirm agent node registration using the server's kubectl client:

```
sudo k3s kubectl get nodes
```

A healthy cluster will list all server and agent nodes with status `Ready`. Nodes may initially appear as `NotReady` as components initialize; this typically resolves in under a minute.

Common Troubleshooting Scenarios

- **Node Not Ready:** If nodes remain in the `NotReady` state, investigate the following:

    - Network connectivity on TCP ports 6443 (Kubernetes API) and 8472 (Flannel VXLAN) must be open between nodes.

    - Firewall rules may block required traffic; adjust with appropriate policies.

- Review K3s logs with `sudo journalctl -u k3s` or `sudo journalctl -u k3s-agent` for errors.

- **Token or Authentication Failures:** Ensure the token is copied correctly without trailing spaces or newlines. Misconfiguration causes agent connection failures.

- **Insufficient Resources:** K3s minimal requirements include at least 512 MB RAM and 1 CPU core for a single-node setup. Resource starvation may cause service crashes.

- **Conflicting Dependencies:** On systems with existing Kubernetes installations or container runtimes, port conflicts or resource clashes can occur. Consider isolating K3s environments or using virtual machines.

Alternative Installation Methods

While the install script covers typical use cases efficiently, manual installation is available for specialized scenarios:

- **Binary Download:** Directly download the K3s binary from the GitHub releases page, place it under `/usr/local/bin`, then manually start with appropriate options.

- **Containerized Deployment:** Run K3s components inside containers, offering control over environment and dependencies.

- **Helm Charts and Ansible Playbooks:** Useful for automated provisioning in CI/CD pipelines or large-scale environments.

Securing the Cluster Post-Installation

After achieving the running state, it is prudent to consider basic security hardening:

- Change the default node-token to a complex secret, generated and distributed securely.

- Limit external access to the Kubernetes API server using firewall rules or VPN tunnels.

- Employ role-based access control (RBAC) policies to restrict cluster resource permissions.

- Enable encryption-at-rest for etcd data stores by configuring K3s with encryption keys.

These measures are critical before transitioning from experimentation to production or multi-tenant usage.

Summary of Quickstart Workflow

1. Run the install script on a designated server node.

2. Copy the k3s.yaml file for CLI interaction.

3. Obtain the agent node token from the server.

4. On each agent node, execute the install script referencing the server and token.

5. Verify all nodes report as Ready via kubectl.

6. Troubleshoot using logs, token validation, and network checks as necessary.

7. Consider post-installation security configuration.

This streamlined approach enables practitioners to bootstrap functional K3s clusters rapidly, providing a robust foundation for deploying containerized applications and exploring the Kubernetes ecosystem with minimal overhead.

2.2. HA Cluster Topologies and External Datastore Support

High availability (HA) cluster architectures are pivotal in minimizing downtime and ensuring continuous service operation in distributed systems. Architecting these clusters requires a thorough understanding of both the in-built datastore options and external datastore integrations such as etcd, MySQL, and PostgreSQL. Each approach influences system topology, failover strategies, and operational resilience in distinct ways.

HA clusters with in-built datastores typically leverage a tightly coupled architecture where the cluster management system embeds the data storage layer. This often uses consensus algorithms—Raft or Paxos—to maintain consistency across nodes. Such designs commonly result in symmetric, peer-to-peer topologies where each node holds a replica of the state, enabling rapid leader election and seamless failover.

In these topologies, the cluster state or metadata is evenly distributed, and every node participates in quorum formation. Failover mechanisms are typically automatic and fast, with detection of node failure triggering leader election among remaining nodes without external dependencies. The downside lies in limited scalability and flexibility; as node count increases, quorum latencies and storage overheads grow, impacting performance under burst load.

A classical example is an in-built multi-node etcd cluster, where the data store replicas concurrently maintain cluster configuration and service discovery data. The replication is synchronous, ensuring strong consistency. A typical three-node setup requires a majority of nodes (two) to operate, facilitating tolerance for a single node failure without service disruption:

```
etcdctl member list
1d1d1d1d1d1d1d1d: name=node1 peerURLs=http://10.0.0.1:2380
    clientURLs=http://10.0.0.1:2379 isLeader=true
```

```
2e2e2e2e2e2e2e2e: name=node2 peerURLs=http://10.0.0.2:2380
    clientURLs=http://10.0.0.2:2379 isLeader=false
3f3f3f3f3f3f3f3f: name=node3 peerURLs=http://10.0.0.3:2380
    clientURLs=http://10.0.0.3:2379 isLeader=false
```

```
OUTPUT:
1d1d1d1d1d1d1d1d: name=node1 isLeader=true
2e2e2e2e2e2e2e2e: name=node2 isLeader=false
3f3f3f3f3f3f3f3f: name=node3 isLeader=false
```

Adopting external datastores like MySQL or PostgreSQL introduces a distinct HA cluster topology centered on decoupling the datastore from application nodes. This approach enables leveraging mature, feature-rich database systems with robust replication and failover capabilities but necessitates careful coordination between application clusters and database replication states.

The external datastore typically resides on a separate HA cluster or replicated instance group. The application cluster nodes act as clients, querying the datastore through network protocols or middleware layers. This separation enables horizontal scaling of compute resources independently from data storage, but also introduces network latency and potential consistency challenges, especially in strongly consistent environments.

For example, PostgreSQL HA setups often employ asynchronous streaming replication supplemented with automated failover tools such as Patroni or PgBouncer. A common topology entails a single primary node handling all write operations, with one or more replicas asynchronously replicating changes:

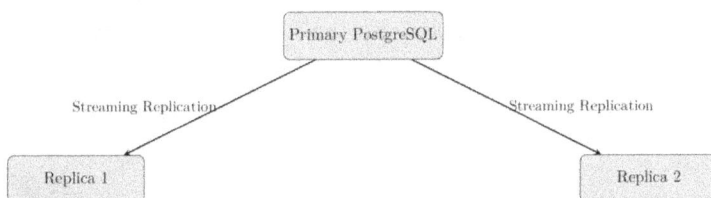

Failover strategies require orchestrated detection of primary failure, promotion of a replica to primary, and reconfiguration of clients. This chain of events adds complexity and time to recovery but benefits from leveraging specialized database failover and backup tools which offer fine-grained control over data durability and consistency.

The choice between in-built and external datastores hinges on system requirements for consistency, scalability, and administrative complexity. Key differentiators include:

- **Topology and Scalability**: In-built datastores enforce a rigid consensus cluster where all nodes participate equally, best suited for small-to-medium clusters requiring strong consistency. External datastores decouple data from compute, facilitating elastic scaling but requiring complex coordination.

- **Failover Mechanisms**: In-built systems leverage automatic leader election and quorum-based failover, minimizing downtime by tightly coupling state management with cluster control. External datastores rely on external failover orchestrators or manual promotion processes, which may lead to longer failover durations but allow use of sophisticated replication features.

- **Operational Complexity**: In-built datastores simplify deployment and upgrades by embedding coordination logic within the cluster but limit flexibility. External datastores demand additional tooling for replication monitoring, failover automation, and backup, increasing operational overhead but improving resilience against data corruption and operational errors.

Best practices for resilient deployments include:

- **Quorum Configuration**: Always configure an odd number of nodes with quorum majority to avoid split-brain scenarios in in-built datastore clusters.

- **Replication Lag Monitoring**: In external datastore setups, continuously monitor replication lag and implement alerts to detect and mitigate stale replicas.

- **Automated Failover**: Employ robust failover automation tools compatible with the datastore to minimize recovery time and human intervention.

- **Network Partition Considerations**: Design cluster topologies to tolerate network partitions by placing nodes across multiple availability zones while ensuring minimal latency.

- **Consistent Backup and Restore**: Implement regular backups and tested restore procedures accounting for the datastore's replication state and cluster consistency requirements.

Architecting HA clusters with either in-built or external datastores involves trade-offs in topology design, failover dynamics, and operational complexity. Selecting the appropriate datastore strategy aligned with application SLA and operational expertise determines the cluster's ability to maintain availability and consistency in real-world failure scenarios.

2.3. Automated Provisioning and Configuration Management

Automating the deployment and configuration of lightweight Kubernetes clusters such as K3s is essential for achieving consistency, repeatability, and scalability in production-grade environments.

This section discusses the orchestration of K3s clusters using Infrastructure as Code (IaC) tools including Ansible, Terraform, and cloud-init, emphasizing effective integration strategies, parameterization, and cluster state management at scale.

Terraform enables declarative management of cloud and on-premises infrastructure, providing an abstraction layer to define compute, networking, and storage resources needed for K3s clusters. Providers for AWS, Azure, Google Cloud, and bare-metal platforms allow provisioning of underlying host instances in a predictable manner.

A typical Terraform configuration for a K3s cluster includes resources such as virtual machines, security groups, and network interfaces. Parameterization via variables allows users to customize cluster node count, instance types, and region locations without altering the core infrastructure code. For example:

```
variable "node_count" {
  default = 3
}

resource "aws_instance" "k3s_node" {
  count         = var.node_count
  ami           = "ami-0abcdef1234567890"
  instance_type = "t3.medium"

  tags = {
    Name = "k3s-node-${count.index}"
  }
}
```

Terraform inherently manages resource dependencies, ensuring that cluster prerequisites such as networking and storage are ready before node allocation. Additionally, its state file provides a single source of truth to track resource changes over time, facilitating drift detection and incremental updates necessary for cluster lifecycle management.

Cloud-init scripts complement Terraform's resource provisioning by automating initial OS-level setup and software installation during machine bootstrapping. Embedding executable shell commands or configurations in user data allows unattended and idempotent installation of the K3s binary, setting of system parameters, and joining nodes into a cluster.

A typical cloud-init snippet configures a node to act as either a server or agent within the K3s cluster:

```
#cloud-config
runcmd:
  - curl -sfL https://get.k3s.io | INSTALL_K3S_VERSION="v1.26.5+
    k3s1" sh -
  - systemctl enable k3s
  - systemctl start k3s
```

Advanced cloud-init templates support fetching configuration files or secrets via secure channels, setting up system limits, and configuring firewalls-all declaratively and reproducibly. Using cloud-init avoids manual SSH interaction, significantly reducing provisioning time and errors.

Ansible bridges the gap between infrastructure provisioning and operational configuration by executing configuration playbooks across clusters post-provisioning. Leveraging its agentless SSH mechanism and extensive module library, Ansible ensures the desired K3s state, node join parameters, and supplemental tooling are consistently applied.

A sample Ansible playbook for K3s deployment centralizes cluster parameters and leverages templating to generate configuration files:

```
- hosts: k3s_servers
  become: yes
  vars:
    k3s_version: "v1.26.5+k3s1"
    k3s_token: "supersecrettoken"
  tasks:
    - name: Download and install K3s
      shell: curl -sfL https://get.k3s.io | INSTALL_K3S_VERSION
      ="{{ k3s_version }}" sh -s - server --token {{ k3s_token }}
      args:
        creates: /usr/local/bin/k3s
```

```
- name: Ensure K3s is running
  systemd:
    name: k3s
    state: started
    enabled: yes
```

Parameterization within Ansible playbooks enables flexible cluster customization, such as distinct roles for servers and agents or variable control-plane endpoints. Combining inventory files and group variables allows scalable management of heterogeneous clusters.

For comprehensive end-to-end automation, Terraform is best utilized to provision the infrastructure layer (nodes, networks, firewalls), while cloud-init handles boot-time OS and package configuration. Ansible complements this by performing post-boot configuration, cluster initialization, and application deployment.

A typical workflow incorporates Terraform outputs as dynamic inventory sources in Ansible, enabling seamless coordination of these toolchains. For example:

- Terraform provisions virtual machines and outputs IP addresses.

- Ansible retrieves these IP addresses as inventory targets.

- Ansible executes cluster bootstrap scripts, assigns roles, and installs additional components.

Automation pipelines, often implemented through CI/CD tools such as Jenkins or GitLab CI, orchestrate these workflows, enabling continuous delivery of infrastructure and cluster configuration with minimal human intervention.

Parameterizing cluster configuration is a crucial aspect of automation, ensuring reusable, modular IaC and configuration templates. Common approaches include:

- **Hierarchical Variable Files**: Separate base configuration from environment-specific overrides (e.g., dev, staging, production).

- **Secret Management Integration**: Reference external vaults, such as HashiCorp Vault or cloud-native secret managers, for sensitive data like cluster tokens.

- **Role-Based Configuration**: Differentiate node parameters according to roles (server, agent, ingress) or availability zones for fault tolerance.

State management at scale becomes challenging as cluster size and node heterogeneity increase. Key practices to manage cluster state in automated environments include:

- **Immutable Infrastructure**: Treat nodes as ephemeral and replace rather than modify in-place, reducing configuration drift risk.

- **Consistent State Files**: Use version-controlled Terraform state storage backed by remote backends (e.g., S3, Consul) with state locking to avoid concurrent inconsistencies.

- **Idempotent Playbooks and Scripts**: Ensure all configuration management code can be safely re-executed without adverse effects.

- **Health Checks and Drift Detection**: Integrate monitoring to detect node misconfigurations or failures and trigger automated remediation workflows.

As cluster size grows, automation tools must adapt to the complexities of multiple data centers, varied operating environments, and differing hardware profiles. Strategies include:

- **Dynamic Inventory and Configuration**: Automate inventory discovery using cloud APIs or DNS SRV records instead of static lists.

- **Parallel Execution and Throttling**: Tune Ansible concurrency settings to balance speed and system resource limits.

- **Modular IaC Components**: Decompose Terraform and Ansible scripts into reusable modules or roles that can be composed for varying deployment topologies.

- **Monitoring and Reporting Integration**: Use automation to dynamically update dashboards and state repositories for operational visibility.

Through deliberate integration of Terraform, cloud-init, and Ansible, combined with robust parameterization and state management strategies, organizations can achieve fully automated, consistent, and scalable K3s cluster deployments aligned with modern DevOps workflows.

2.4. K3sup, Rancher, and Alternative Initializers

Efficient management of K3s clusters often requires tooling that abstracts and automates many lifecycle operations, ranging from initial node provisioning to cluster upgrades and node scaling. While manual installation via shell scripts or Ansible playbooks offers full control, purpose-built tools such as k3sup and Rancher provide streamlined workflows designed to reduce operational overhead with standardized safeguards. This section examines these tools, comparing their capabilities, typical usage patterns, and tradeoffs to enable informed decision-making about cluster initialization and management strategies.

k3sup (pronounced "ketchup") is a compact, open-source command line utility built specifically for bootstrapping K3s clusters from a local machine to remote hosts over SSH. It focuses on simplicity and minimal dependencies, relying on direct SSH connectivity and standard Linux utilities on the target nodes. The fundamental workflow of k3sup typically involves executing a single command to install or join a node:

```
k3sup install --ip <SERVER_IP> --user <USER>
```

This command remotely downloads the official K3s binary and executes a tailored installer script, automatically configuring the server node with sensible defaults such as embedded etcd and containerd for runtime. For worker nodes, a similarly straightforward command pattern allows seamless cluster joining by fetching the join token and necessary certificates from the server node:

```
k3sup join --ip <WORKER_IP> --server-ip <SERVER_IP> --user <USER>
```

The primary strength of k3sup lies in its minimal configuration surface and rapid cluster deployment capability. It is ideally suited for small to medium clusters where administrators prioritize speed and simplicity over granular customization. Since it directly invokes the upstream K3s installer, the tool reflects Kubernetes project updates promptly, ensuring compatibility with new K3s releases.

However, k3sup abstracts away certain advanced configuration options, such as intricate network overlays and fine-tuned resource control, requiring supplementary manual steps or a layered configuration management system for highly customized setups. Additionally, k3sup does not maintain operational state or perform ongoing cluster management; it is best viewed as a bootstrap utility rather than a full lifecycle platform.

In contrast, Rancher embodies a comprehensive cluster management system aimed at larger-scale Kubernetes installations, including K3s clusters, and multi-cluster environments. Delivered as a Kubernetes-native application hosted on a management cluster, Rancher provides a graphical user interface (GUI) alongside extensive APIs to handle provisioning, policy enforcement, upgrades, monitoring, and multi-tenant access control.

Rancher's installation and node initialization tooling addresses multiple infrastructure providers and cluster types through an abstraction layer called *cluster drivers*. These drivers enable Rancher to orchestrate provisioning on bare metal, cloud platforms, and virtual machines, applying K3s as one of the supported Kubernetes distributions. Cluster creation workflows in Rancher involve defining node templates and node pools with configurable roles—control plane, worker, etcd—allowing declarative management of the cluster state:

- **Node templates:** Specify OS images, network configurations, and Docker or container runtimes.

- **Node pools:** Define grouping and scaling of nodes with shared characteristics.

- **Provisioning via agents:** Nodes execute Rancher's agent, reporting status and applying lifecycle commands issued from the management server.

This model enables continuous reconciliation of cluster state, automatic handling of upgrade strategies with minimal downtime, and granular RBAC tailored for operational teams. The Rancher GUI greatly reduces the barrier to entry for users less familiar with Kubernetes internals, integrating monitoring and alerting tools as part of the management experience.

The tradeoff with Rancher lies in the added complexity and resource overhead of running a dedicated management cluster, as well as the initial learning curve associated with its rich feature set. Organizations with multi-cluster needs or requiring integrated Kubernetes platform services often find Rancher's capabilities indispensable, whereas small single-cluster deployments may find the additional layer superfluous.

Alternative initialization approaches fall between these extremes. Custom scripts and configuration management frameworks such as Ansible, Terraform, or Helm charts can encode bespoke procedures reflecting precise organizational policies and infrastructure specifics. These methods enable complete flexibility, allowing pre-installation validation, complex network setup, configuration of external storage backends, or integration with internal identity and certificate authorities. However, these benefits come with increased maintenance burden and risk of configuration drift.

An emerging pattern involves combining k3sup's fast bootstrap with configuration management applied post-install to customize cluster behavior, thus harnessing the agility of simple installation with the rigor of institutional policies. Similarly, Rancher's ability to integrate externally provisioned nodes allows hybrid approaches where foundational node setup occurs outside Rancher, with subsequent enrollment into Rancher's management plane.

Determining the optimal lifecycle management strategy requires weighing several criteria:

- **Cluster scale and complexity:** Larger clusters or multi-cluster fleets favor Rancher's robust management features.

- **Operational expertise:** Teams with strong Kubernetes knowledge may prefer scripting solutions or k3sup for control and immediacy.

- **Infrastructure heterogeneity:** Rancher's multi-provider abstraction suits heterogeneous environments; k3sup performs best with homogeneous Linux hosts reachable via SSH.

- **Upgrade and lifecycle policies:** Rancher supports declarative upgrades and policy enforcement; manual and script-based approaches require custom development of these processes.

- **Resource constraints:** Lightweight edge environments with minimal overhead align well with k3sup installations.

k3sup offers a pragmatic, minimalistic bootstrap mechanism emphasizing rapid K3s cluster creation with limited post-install management. Rancher targets comprehensive, scalable Kubernetes operations supporting multi-cluster governance and lifecycle orchestration through a full-featured platform. Alternative methods via custom tooling continue to provide maximal flexibility at the cost of engineering and operational effort. Understanding these trade-offs and operational contexts empowers Kubernetes practitioners to select a cluster initialization and management approach aligned to their technical requirements and organizational maturity.

2.5. Bootstrapping in Constrained Environments

Deploying Kubernetes in constrained environments necessitates a tailored approach to address limitations intrinsic to edge hardware, IoT devices, and networks with restricted bandwidth or intermittent connectivity. K3s, a lightweight Kubernetes distribution, is specifically designed to facilitate orchestration under stringent resource constraints. This section examines methodologies for bootstrapping K3s clusters in such environments and elucidates adaptations, best practices, and common pitfalls associated with ARM architectures, limited memory footprints, and network variability.

The fundamental challenge in constrained environments arises from the disparity between Kubernetes' original design—oriented towards data centers with abundant compute and storage resources—and the austere resource profile of edge devices. K3s mitigates this by packaging essential Kubernetes components into a minimal binary, reducing memory and CPU consumption, and by eliminating non-critical features. Yet, effective deployment demands further considerations.

Adapting to ARM Architectures

Edge and IoT devices predominantly utilize ARM processors due to superior power efficiency and cost-effectiveness. Although K3s supports ARM64 and ARMv7 architectures, certain nuances must be addressed:

- **Container Runtime Compatibility**: K3s defaults to containerd, which supports ARM; however, ensuring that containerd binaries and container images are ARM-compatible is critical. Custom container image builds may be necessary, as mainstream images often target x86 architectures. Multi-architecture manifest lists facilitate automatic selection of the appropriate image variant.

- **Operating System and Kernel Requirements**: Lightweight Linux distributions such as Alpine, Ubuntu Core, and BalenaOS suit ARM devices but require kernel versions that support necessary container and networking primitives. Kernel features such as cgroups v2 and overlayfs are often prerequisites, and older kernels may necessitate configuration adjustments or upgrades.

- **Cross-Compilation and Toolchains**: Building K3s or ancillary components for ARM may require cross-compilation toolchains. It is advisable to use official multi-arch releases or container image registries with built-in ARM support to avoid complex build processes.

Handling Limited Memory and CPU Resources

Constrained devices typically present severe limits on memory (often below 1 GB) and modest CPU capabilities. K3s is engineered to operate with as little as 512 MB of RAM, but careful tuning is essential:

- **Disabling Non-Essential Features**: K3s allows disabling telemetry, service load balancer, or cloud controller integrations during installation, conserving valuable memory and CPU cycles.

- **Optimizing Kubernetes Component Flags**: The embedded kube-apiserver, kube-scheduler, and kube-controller-manager can be fine-tuned via command-line flags to lower resource usage (e.g., reducing cache sizes or disabling admission controllers not requisite for the use case).

- **Memory Swapping and Overcommit Settings**: Since swap can exacerbate latency, disabling swap or adjusting Linux overcommit parameters helps maintain responsiveness.

- **Lightweight Networking Plugins**: Using minimalist CNI plugins such as Flannel in host-gw mode or Cilium with BPF, configured to minimize overhead, can prevent networking from dominating resource usage.

Managing Intermittent Network Connectivity

Network variability is inherent in edge environments. Unlike data centers with persistent, low-latency connections, IoT and edge devices often experience frequent disconnections or constrained upstream bandwidth. Several techniques and practices facilitate cluster stability:

- **Control Plane Node Placement**: For highly intermittent connectivity, deploying control plane components locally on edge hardware is preferable to relying on distant data center nodes. K3s supports running single-node clusters optimized for offline operation.

- **Using Embedded SQLite Instead of etcd**: The default storage backend for small clusters in K3s is SQLite, reducing the complexity and network requirements of distributed etcd clusters. This configuration is more robust to network partitions and requires less synchronization traffic.

- **Cluster Agent and Server Communication**: K3s separates server and agent components, allowing agents to buffer and retry communications during outages. Configuring appropriate heartbeat intervals and timeouts is necessary to balance responsiveness and false-positive failure detection.

- **Image and Binary Caching**: Pre-pulling container images and binaries or deploying local registries mitigates reliance on network availability. Air-gapped environments benefit from image mirroring strategies, automated synchronization through low-bandwidth channels, or update bundling.

- **Service Mesh and Sidecar Proxies**: While service meshes add overhead, minimal sidecar proxies configured to buffer or queue requests can smooth transient disconnections.

Best Practices in Security and Persistence

Bootstrapping K3s in constrained environments must not compromise security or data persistence:

- **Secure Bootstrapping Tokens**: Due to limited interaction windows, token generation and rotation should be automated and integrated (e.g., via pre-shared keys or trusted provisioning servers). Tokens must be managed with caution on edge devices, which often lack physical security.

- **TLS Certificates Management**: Embedded certificate authorities simplify cluster security but may impose rotation overheads. Lightweight certificate management approaches, coupled with short-lived credentials, reduce attack surface.

- **Persistent Storage Options**: Given limited local storage and intermittent network, the choice of storage backend for persistent data (such as logs or application state) warrants careful design. Local storage class implementations using embedded flash or NVMe devices must account for wear-leveling and failure modes.

- **Resource Quotas and Limits**: Restricting container resource consumption is even more critical in constrained environments to avoid starvation and cascading failures.

Common Pitfalls and Their Mitigation

Several recurrent issues emerge when deploying K3s on constrained hardware:

- **Overloading Devices Beyond Capacity**: Attempting to run full Kubernetes features or resource-heavy workloads on minimal hardware leads to instability. Profiling and benchmarking prior to deployment help avoid this.

- **Neglecting Architecture-Specific Image Compatibility**: Using default or unofficial container images not compiled for ARM architectures causes deployment failures or runtime crashes.

- **Ignoring Network Partitioning Effects**: Assuming continuous control plane availability in unstable networks leads to failed probes and pod evictions. Designing clusters for partition tolerance and failover is imperative.

- **Insufficient Logging and Monitoring**: Resource constraints can tempt disabling telemetry but this complicates troubleshooting. Employ lightweight metrics exporters and centralized aggregation where feasible.

- **Improper Configuration Management**: Manual configuration of myriad devices introduces configuration drift and human error. Employ infrastructure-as-code tools adapted for edge environments to maintain consistency.

Together, these adaptations and best practices empower robust bootstrapping and operation of K3s clusters in constrained and heterogeneous environments. Selecting appropriate hardware, optimizing software components for the specific constraints, and accounting for network volatility are essential to unlocking the potential of Kubernetes orchestration at the edge and in IoT systems.

2.6. Networking and Security During Bootstrap

Securely initializing a K3s cluster requires comprehensive attention to networking and security controls from the moment the cluster comes online. Since K3s is often deployed in lightweight or edge environments with varying threat models, establishing a robust security foundation during bootstrap mitigates risks stemming from default configurations and exposure of critical endpoints. This section delineates best practices for hardening network policies, TLS certificate management, infrastructure firewall settings, and securing startup service endpoints such as ServiceLB.

The first layer of security involves defining explicit network policies that restrict communication between pods and external entities. K3s supports standard Kubernetes NetworkPolicy resources, enabling fine-grained control over ingress and egress traffic within the cluster. Before workloads are deployed, it is essential to:

- Create a default deny-all policy for both ingress and egress at the namespace level:

```
apiVersion: networking.k8s.io/v1
kind: NetworkPolicy
metadata:
  name: default-deny-all
  namespace: default
spec:
  podSelector: {}
  policyTypes:
  - Ingress
  - Egress
```

- Layer on minimal allow rules tailored for core system components and essential services, such as kube-apiserver, CoreDNS, and metrics endpoints. For example, allow only port 6443 traffic from control plane nodes and restricted pod CIDRs.

This approach blocks lateral movement and limits the attack surface during bootstrap. Applying network policies from the outset enforces a principle of least privilege and is critical because K3s deploys several system pods automatically (like CoreDNS, local-path provisioner, and Traefik or alternative ingress controllers) that can otherwise communicate freely.

TLS certificates are foundational to securing communication channels within the cluster. K3s simplifies certificate generation and lifecycle management internally, but explicit management remains essential for ensuring cryptographic integrity during bootstrap and subsequent operation.

- **Pre-generate or securely provision certificates:** Where possible, generate cluster certificates externally using a trusted Certificate Authority (CA) and supply them during installation to eliminate reliance on ephemeral self-signed certificates. This practice improves auditability and trust establishment.

- **Enable certificate rotation:** Configure automatic TLS certificate rotation for kubelet and API server components to minimize risks from compromised or expired credentials. K3s versions post-1.20 support built-in rotation mechanisms that should be enabled explicitly.

- **Secure certificate storage:** Utilize secure storage backends to protect certificates and private keys. Running the cluster control plane on hardware with Trusted Platform Modules (TPM) or dedicated Hardware Security Modules (HSM) enhances key security significantly.

Certificate files should never reside on publicly accessible filesystems or shared volumes without encryption. When using K3s's default embedded CA, administrators must secure the server's file system and control access tightly.

Cluster nodes should be protected by well-defined infrastructure-level firewall rules to control external access and internal communication. During bootstrap, the firewall must:

- **Limit inbound access to the API server:** Restrict access to kube-apiserver's HTTPS port (default 6443) to trusted IP ranges associated with cluster administrators and control plane components.

- **Control node-to-node traffic:** Depending on the CNI plugin and cluster topology, allow necessary intra-node communications for pod networking (commonly UDP ports for VXLAN or Flannel) while blocking unnecessary exposure from untrusted networks.

- **Permit essential service ports for cluster components:** Open only service ports required by system pods such as the service load balancer (ServiceLB), metrics, and DNS services. Ports like 8472 for Flannel VXLAN encapsulation or 10250 for kubelet APIs should be accessible only within the cluster network.

A sample minimal iptables-based firewall rule set might be:

```
# Allow kube-apiserver access from control plane IP
iptables -A INPUT -p tcp -s 10.0.0.0/24 --dport 6443 -j ACCEPT

# Allow kubelet API communication within cluster
iptables -A INPUT -p tcp -s 10.0.0.0/16 --dport 10250 -j ACCEPT

# Block all other inbound by default
iptables -P INPUT DROP
```

Complementing cluster-level firewall rules with virtual private cloud (VPC) security groups or cloud provider network ACLs ensures defense in depth.

ServiceLB deployed by K3s provides built-in load balancing capabilities for Services of type LoadBalancer. Although convenient, it exposes critical endpoints that must be secured:

- **Restrict external ServiceLB access:** By default, ServiceLB listens on all interfaces. During bootstrap, configure ServiceLB to bind only to trusted network interfaces or assign IP ranges that are inaccessible from untrusted networks. This can be achieved by setting the `--node-external-ip` parameter or firewall filtering.

- **Authentication and authorization:** ServiceLB endpoints should be protected by network layer controls and optionally integrated with Kubernetes RBAC policies to prevent unauthorized service exposure or modification.

- **Monitor and limit metrics and debug ports:** System components often expose health, metrics, or debug endpoints locally. Restrict access to these by firewall rules or via Kubernetes Admission Controllers to minimize attack vectors during cluster bootstrap.

- **Employ ephemeral or dynamically allocated addresses cautiously:** Avoid configurations in which ephemeral IPs for ServiceLB allow unexpected external access.

Summarizing best practices for a hardened K3s bootstrap:

1. Deploy default deny-all Kubernetes NetworkPolicy resources in all namespaces to isolate workloads and control traffic explicitly.

2. Supply pre-generated TLS certificates signed by enterprise CAs or trusted authorities during K3s installation. Enable certificate rotation features early.

3. Configure infrastructure firewalls and cloud security groups to restrict API server ingress, node communication, and service ports strictly to trusted IPs and interfaces.

4. Harden ServiceLB endpoints by binding to internal interfaces, restricting exposure with firewall rules, and controlling access through RBAC.

5. Secure storage and access to TLS private keys and cluster credentials with strong filesystem permissions or hardware security modules.

6. Regularly audit network flows and running processes during and immediately after bootstrap to detect unintended open ports or abnormal traffic patterns.

7. Integrate logging and monitoring solutions early to capture startup events and anomalies, supporting timely incident response.

Implementing these precautions during bootstrap sets a strong security baseline that scales as cluster complexity grows. Ensuring that network isolation, cryptographic credentials, and access controls are robust from first boot directly fortifies the cluster against lateral intrusions, privilege escalation, and information leakage. Consequently, careful orchestration of networking and security during bootstrap significantly reduces the operational risk profile of K3s clusters in production and edge deployments.

Chapter 3

K3s Deep Architecture and Internals

What makes K3s astonishingly lean yet remarkably powerful? This chapter journeys under the hood, dissecting K3s's core architectural strategies and technical shortcuts. Discover how design decisions, clever packaging, and streamlined subsystems transform Kubernetes into a lightweight engine for modern, distributed systems.

3.1. Component Packaging and Binary Design

K3s achieves its hallmark compactness by consolidating Kubernetes and essential dependencies into a single statically compiled binary. This design philosophy significantly reduces the operational footprint while sustaining the robustness and extensibility expected from a Kubernetes distribution. The consolidation process involves meticulous pruning of non-essential Kubernetes components alongside the integration of supporting system services, striking a balance between minimalism and functional completeness.

At the core of K3s's packaging strategy lies the concept of multi-platform builds. Given the heterogeneity of modern hardware architectures-ranging from x86_64 and ARMv7 to ARM64-K3s employs a build pipeline capable of producing binaries that are both architecture-agnostic and optimized for targeted platforms. This is achieved using Go's inherent cross-compilation capabilities, which enable static linking of all dependencies into a single executable. The static compilation approach eradicates the need for external dynamic libraries at runtime, thus eliminating version mismatches and dependency hell common in traditional Kubernetes deployments.

The build process begins with a controlled compilation environment where specific versions of Kubernetes components and auxiliary tools are selected and merged. This environment leverages Go modules to enforce consistent dependency versions across the entire stack. Each included component is configured to disable or remove optional plugins and features that are superfluous to K3s's intended use cases, primarily edge and resource-constrained environments. For example, cloud-provider integrations and heavy storage plugins are excluded unless explicitly enabled.

Static compilation is performed using go build with flags that enforce position-independent code and disable certain runtime features to optimize size. The final binary integrates critical Kubernetes components-including the API server, controller manager, scheduler, and kubelet-alongside embedded versions of container runtimes like containerd. This fusion avoids separate installations and reduces I/O overhead. The embedded containerd version is streamlined, lacking features such as the full OCI runtime suite, yet retaining compatibility with required container standards.

A key advantage of the unified binary design is the simplification of upgrade and rollback workflows. Since Kubernetes components and dependencies are bundled together, version skew between API server and kubelet or controller manager is inherently prevented. However, this monolithic approach necessitates careful curation of included features. To achieve this, the K3s development team conducts rigorous security and functionality auditing, identifying redundant services that can be pruned without compromising operational integrity.

Pruning predominantly targets legacy or seldom-used Kubernetes components and optional services. For instance, etcd is replaced as the default datastore by SQLite for single-node setups, eliminating the need for running and managing an external etcd cluster in resource-constrained environments. Similarly, auxiliary controllers that handle features like custom resource definitions for ephemeral volumes or in-tree cloud provider controllers are either stripped or conditionally compiled out. This selective removal is codified through Go build tags that exclude code paths associated with these features during compilation.

In addition to code pruning, K3s optimizes networking components by substituting the default Kubernetes Container Network Interface (CNI) plugins with lightweight alternatives. The binary embeds a simpler CNI plugin that supports common network configurations without the overhead of multiple plugin installations or complex configurations. This networking simplification results in lower memory and CPU usage while preserving compliance with the Kubernetes networking model.

The innovation of embedding multiple services in a coherent single binary extends to internal orchestration. K3s internally coordinates the lifecycle of embedded components through a lightweight controller framework, which handles initialization, health checks, and dynamic configuration. This contrasts with the conventional model where separate system daemons and containers manage these tasks independently. The unified approach reduces interprocess communication latency and simplifies monitoring and logging pipelines by funneling outputs through centralized interfaces.

Despite the compactness and pruning, K3s maintains extensibility through its support for modular add-ons. These add-ons, which include Helm controllers, CoreDNS, and service meshes, are deployed as standard Kubernetes manifests or Helm charts atop the minimal base cluster. The modularity is preserved without inflating the binary since these components remain decoupled and externally managed, providing flexibility to scale functionality up or down depending on the deployment scenario.

K3s's component packaging and binary design exemplify a thoughtful synthesis of multi-platform static compilation, selective feature pruning, and single-binary integration. Its approach delivers a Kubernetes distribution tailored for constrained environments without sacrificing essential orchestration features. This model not only simplifies deployment and reduces dependency complexity but also enhances security posture through minimized attack surfaces inherent in fewer running processes and dependencies.

3.2. Integrated Add-ons and System Services

Within modern container orchestration platforms, integrated add-ons and system services play a pivotal role in operational stability, system observability, and application connectivity. Bundled by default, key services such as Traefik, CoreDNS, and the metrics server form the backbone of the cluster's internal networking, service discovery, and resource monitoring capabilities. The rationale behind their inclusion, as well as the mechanisms for customization or replacement, reflect a deliberate balance between out-of-the-box simplicity and platform extensibility.

Traefik, a dynamic reverse proxy and load balancer, is often chosen as the default ingress controller in lightweight Kubernetes distributions. Its declarative model, automatic configuration through Kubernetes ingress resources, and native support for multiple protocols streamline the exposure of services to external traffic. The integration of Traefik reduces the operational burden on users who might otherwise need to deploy and configure ingress controllers manually. Traefik's dynamic routing capabilities allow seamless management of encrypted traffic via Let's Encrypt integration, thereby providing automatic certificate generation and renewal without additional configuration. However, the choice of Traefik also implies certain defaults-such as embedded routing rules and middleware configurations-that may not fit all advanced use cases. Therefore, clusters typically enable Traefik as a configurable add-on that can be disabled or superseded by custom ingress controllers aligned with specific enterprise requirements.

CoreDNS serves as the default DNS service, replacing the prior kube-dns implementation in many default Kubernetes clusters. It delivers service discovery functionality by resolving internal DNS queries for services, pods, and external names. CoreDNS's modular design, leveraging a plugin-based architecture, enhances performance and extensibility with minimal resource overhead. Its default configuration includes forwarding, cache, hosts, and Kubernetes-specific plugins optimized for cluster operations. Leveraging CoreDNS simplifies name resolution and promotes higher availability via built-in health checking and load balancing features. Clusters enable CoreDNS as a critical system add-on that can be disabled or replaced if alternative DNS services are preferable, although the impact on service discovery should be carefully assessed. For example, swapping CoreDNS for a custom implementation demands ensuring compliance with Kubernetes DNS specifications to prevent resolution failures or latency increases.

The metrics server acts as a resource consumption aggregator, collecting CPU and memory usage statistics from the Kubelet on each node. This data enables horizontal pod autoscaling (HPA), resource quota enforcement, and monitoring through Kubernetes API extensions. The metrics server, while inherently lightweight and designed for minimal performance impact, is critical for maintaining elasticity and efficiency of workloads in production environments. Its integration is predicated on simplicity-allowing users to expend minimal effort deploying and maintaining a core metrics pipeline. Disabling the metrics server removes autoscaling functionality, which may be acceptable for static workload scenarios but limits responsive resource optimization. Substituting the metrics server with more comprehensive telemetry systems, such as Prometheus, is feasible and occasionally necessary for detailed observability, but requires architectural considerations to avoid redundancy or data inconsistency.

Facilitating enablement, disablement, or replacement of these system services is typically managed via declarative cluster configuration files or command-line options exposed by cluster bootstrap tools. For instance, the user may specify flags to disable Traefik ingress or CoreDNS during cluster initialization or patch the cluster's configuration post-deployment to alter service parameters. These mechanisms contribute to flexibility by accommodating diverse deployment scenarios, including air-gapped environments or integrations with external infrastructure components. Importantly, the seamless toggling of bundled services depends on tight integration with cluster lifecycle management, ensuring that dependent controllers, API resources, and cluster add-ons remain aligned.

The implications of these default bundled services extend beyond mere convenience. By standardizing on proven, lightweight components like Traefik, CoreDNS, and the metrics server, distributions reduce the cognitive load on administrators, accelerate cluster readiness, and deliver consistent operational semantics. At the same time, the openness of these components' architectures and their modular enablement models foster extensibility. Users can evolve their cluster infrastructure organically-disabling default add-ons to adopt alternative ingress controllers optimized for advanced protocol support, replacing DNS with custom solutions for specific naming schemes, or integrating more sophisticated monitoring pipelines. This dual dynamic between default simplicity and extensibility recognizes the diverse operational requirements of cloud-native workloads and the need for platforms to serve both novice and expert users.

Bundled services such as Traefik, CoreDNS, and the metrics server embody a strategic blend of default configuration and adaptive potential. Their selection reflects a careful consideration of resource efficiency, functionality coverage, and ecosystem maturity. Through flexible enablement and replacement options, clusters foster both immediate usability and long-term customization, making them foundational components of modern container orchestration frameworks.

3.3. Internal Kubernetes API Changes

K3s, conceived as a lightweight Kubernetes distribution, introduces a series of deliberate internal modifications to the Kubernetes API to optimize for reduced resource consumption, simplified operation, and enhanced suitability for edge and IoT environments. These modifications predominantly involve the customization, streamlining, and selective exclusion of various API objects and functionalities, which inevitably influence both application compatibility and portability.

Fundamentally, the K3s API retains Kubernetes' core structural and behavioral principles, thereby preserving compatibility with standard Kubernetes API clients and tooling. However, to achieve its minimalistic design goals, K3s selectively refactors certain API components and disables or replaces resource-intensive features. This approach ensures a smaller footprint but introduces nuanced deviations from upstream Kubernetes API conventions.

API Object Adjustments and Streamlining

The most prominent alterations concern the API object model, where K3s redefines or omits particular workloads and core resources. For example, the Custom Resource Definitions (CRDs) supported by default are trimmed to exclude less commonly used extensions and experimental APIs that would otherwise increase complexity and memory overhead. Resources pertaining to legacy or rarely utilized controllers such as certain storage classes and ingress controllers are either supplanted by lightweight alternatives or removed entirely.

A critical facet is the built-in consolidation and simplification of the networking APIs. K3s defaults to using a tightly integrated, simplified Container Network Interface (CNI) plugin set, resulting in adjustments to networking-related API fields and interactions. Some network policy capabilities and resource specifications are restricted or modified to align with the streamlined CNI model, which affects how network segmentation and security policies are implemented.

The CoreDNS and metrics server components are customized with API endpoint modifications to reduce resource requirements, leading to subtle changes in Service and EndpointSlice APIs and their management. As a result, the observable behaviors and metrics interfaces exposed by the cluster can vary slightly from standard Kubernetes deployments.

Exclusions and Disabled Functionality

Certain Kubernetes API functionalities are consciously disabled or excluded in K3s. The primary target of these exclusions is the set of features that impose considerable computational or storage demands. For instance, the Default StorageClass is simplified, and support for dynamic volume provisioning through complex CSI drivers is minimized. While basic CSI functionality is retained, some standard volume expansion and snapshotting APIs are disabled or unsupported.

Similarly, API features related to PodSecurityPolicies are removed, aligning with the upstream deprecation trajectory but also reflecting K3s' preference for relying on alternative security mechanisms. StatefulSets, while supported, are deployed with reduced default replicas and simplified reconciliation loops to optimize performance, potentially impacting update and failover behaviors.

The API server itself in K3s is embedded within a single binary, incorporating a modified version of Kubernetes' API server with internal defaults adjusted to disable audit logging and webhook admission controllers by default. This exclusion reduces overhead but requires explicit configuration for advanced admission control mechanisms, influencing how the cluster enforces policy via API extensions.

Impact on Application Compatibility

The cumulative effect of these API changes means that, while most standard Kubernetes workloads deploy transparently on K3s without modification, certain applications that depend on full-fledged API capabilities may require adaptation. Applications leveraging advanced storage features, extensive network policy controls, or requiring specific admission controllers will encounter limitations or necessitate reconfiguration.

The removal or alteration of some CRDs and deprecated APIs mandates verification during application migration to K3s. Ensuring compatibility often involves explicitly specifying alternative supported APIs or refactoring manifests to align with K3s' streamlined resource model. Nevertheless, K3s typically maintains backward compatibility for the majority of workload types, making it suitable for test, edge, and development environments where absolute upstream fidelity is less critical.

Portability Considerations

From a portability standpoint, these internal Kubernetes API changes pose a dual-edged challenge. On one hand, K3s' lightweight API ensures deployment on constrained hardware environments is feasible, thus expanding Kubernetes' applicability spectrum. On the other hand, the customized API model means that applications and operators designed and tested on full Kubernetes distributions such as kubeadm, GKE, or EKS cannot be assumed implicitly portable to K3s clusters.

Careful API compatibility audits and incremental testing become mandatory to maintain portability. Cross-environment deployment pipelines need to incorporate checks that account for K3s' adjusted API surface. This is particularly vital for continuous delivery workflows where manifests must dynamically accommodate differences in available services, API versions, and enabled features.

To mitigate portability friction, the K3s project encourages the use of well-established stable APIs and recommends avoiding deprecated or non-standard extensions during application development. Containerized applications designed with portability in mind-using minimal dependencies on Kubernetes ecosystem extensions-will exhibit smoother transitions between K3s and standard Kubernetes environments.

The internal Kubernetes API changes embodied by K3s represent carefully considered trade-offs focused on performance, resource economy, and operational simplicity. By selectively adjusting, streamlining, and excluding legacy or non-essential Kubernetes features, K3s achieves a remarkably compressed yet functional API environment. Consequently, this tailored API model ensures K3s serves targeted use cases-edge deployments, IoT clusters, and development sandboxes-while maintaining broad compatibility with standard Kubernetes APIs at the core.

Appreciating the scope and nature of these internal API modifications is essential for systems architects and developers aiming to leverage K3s effectively. Understanding which functionalities are altered or absent informs architectural decisions around application design, deployment automation, and cross-platform orchestration strategies, thereby ensuring optimal utilization of K3s' strengths without unintended compatibility pitfalls.

3.4. K3s Agent/Server Model and Node Lifecycle

K3s, as a lightweight Kubernetes distribution, employs a distinct agent/server architecture that optimizes resource usage while maintaining full Kubernetes cluster functionality. This architecture delineates the roles and responsibilities of nodes as either *servers* (control plane nodes) or *agents* (worker nodes), orchestrating communication, cluster state management, and workload scheduling.

At its core, the **K3s server** consolidates the Kubernetes control plane components: the API server, scheduler, controller-manager, and etcd or an embedded datastore such as SQLite by default. This server layer acts as the authoritative source of cluster state and policy enforcement. In contrast, **K3s agents** are responsible primarily for running workloads, executing containers, and maintaining node health information. Agents host the kubelet process and container runtime, providing the compute capacity directed by the server.

Communication between the server and agents is predicated on the Kubernetes API and related protocols, supplemented by K3s-specific enhancements. Agents initiate a secure TLS connection to the server's API endpoint, leveraging shared cluster credentials provisioned during the join process. This client-server architecture underpins the control loop whereby agents continuously report node metrics, status, and events while fetching pod specifications and configuration details from the server.

Node Join Protocol

When a new node is introduced to a K3s cluster, it undergoes a controlled join procedure, which ensures seamless integration and security. The agent node begins by installing the K3s agent component and initiating contact with the server via the provided server URL and shared token or certificate. The join sequence involves the following steps:

- **Authentication and Authorization:** The new agent authenticates using the pre-shared secret or client certificates configured on the server. This ensures that only authorized nodes can join the cluster.

- **Node Registration:** Upon successful authentication, the server registers the new node in its internal state and updates the API server with the corresponding Node object.

- **Initial Configuration Synchronization:** The server transmits cluster configuration parameters, including network overlay information (e.g., Flannel or Canal), taints, labels, and resource quotas relevant to the node.

- **Heartbeat and Health Checks Initiation:** The agent starts periodic heartbeats and status reporting, enabling the control plane to monitor node health continuously.

This join protocol, designed for simplicity and security, allows the cluster to dynamically scale by adding new agents without manual API-level intervention or complex orchestration.

Node Leave and Removal Process

Node departure in K3s can be intentional or unintentional, with procedures adapting accordingly. When an administrator manually removes a node, the server initiates a graceful drain procedure, which evicts running pods, respecting PodDisruptionBudgets to minimize application downtime. The drain sequence proceeds as follows:

- **Mark Node Unschedulable:** The node is cordoned to prevent new pods from scheduling.

- **Pod Eviction:** Running pods are evicted according to Kubernetes policies, with replicas rescheduled onto other healthy nodes.

- **Node Deregistration:** The node's entry is removed from the cluster's etcd-backed state to stop heartbeats and metrics reporting.

In the event of node failure or network partition causing unresponsiveness, the server relies on liveness and readiness probes alongside heartbeat timeouts to detect node unavailability. If a node remains unresponsive past the configured threshold (e.g., five minutes), the control plane considers it lost and initiates pod rescheduling. The defunct node's record will be eventually pruned through automated garbage collection, facilitating cluster contraction without manual cleanup.

Lifecycle Events and Cluster State Transitions

K3s monitors node lifecycle events through the control plane and agent's synchronization loops to maintain cluster coherence. Key lifecycle events include `NodeReady`, `NodeNotReady`, `NodeUnknown`, and custom taints signaling maintenance or draining states. These events are integral to the scheduler's decisions on workload placement and are propagated in real time via the Kubernetes API watch mechanism.

The agents emit health status and resource metrics every heartbeat cycle to the server, enabling proactive identification of performance degradation or failure scenarios. The server aggregates these metrics, integrating them into cluster-wide autoscaling decisions and load balancing adjustments.

Importantly, the lightweight design of K3s—with embedded components and streamlined control plane operations—

optimizes communication overhead. Persistent connections and multiplexed gRPC streams between agents and servers minimize latency and load on cluster networking, ensuring efficient lifecycle event propagation even in resource-constrained environments.

Efficient Cluster Expansion and Contraction in K3s

Cluster scalability in K3s emphasizes swift, reliable node addition and removal with minimal manual configuration. The token-based join model removes dependency on complex certificate generation workflows, reducing time-to-deploy for new agents. Additionally, K3s backend datastores provide rapid synchronization and consistency, facilitating immediate recognition of node state changes across distributed control plane components.

Network overlays in K3s support automatic IP assignment and routing updates as nodes join or leave, enabling pods to communicate transparently without manual network reconfiguration. Such overlay network updates propagate rapidly through agent-server interactions, maintaining cluster connectivity integrity.

Furthermore, K3s supports embedded load balancing and role-based segregation of workloads, allowing server nodes to operate in high-availability configurations or as lightweight single-node clusters depending on deployment scenarios. This flexibility ensures that cluster expansion or contraction can be tailored precisely to operational requirements without compromising reliability.

In summary, the K3s agent/server model leverages secure, lightweight protocols and efficient control loops to manage node lifecycles dynamically. Its node join and leave processes enforce secure, consistent state management, while lifecycle event tracking ensures real-time responsiveness. Together, these mechanisms empower K3s clusters to scale fluidly with minimal overhead, making it a compelling choice for edge, IoT, and resource-constrained Kubernetes deployments.

3.5. Database Storage Subsystem

The database storage subsystem forms a critical backbone in Kubernetes distributions like K3s, where maintaining cluster state consistency and availability are paramount. K3s employs an architecture that supports multiple storage backends, each optimized for different deployment scenarios and state synchronization requirements. The storage options typically range from lightweight embedded databases such as SQLite to more robust distributed key-value stores such as etcd, alongside traditional relational databases like MySQL and PostgreSQL.

Embedded SQLite is the default storage backend for K3s, particularly suited for single-node clusters or development environments. Its lightweight and serverless architecture allows for rapid initialization without dependency overhead. SQLite persists cluster state in a local file system with ACID guarantees, handling transactional consistency through write-ahead logging. However, SQLite lacks native networked state synchronization, making it unsuitable for multi-node clusters needing strong consistency across distributed components. Thus, K3s extends SQLite functionality by introducing a distributed SQLite synchronization layer via a consensus protocol, Raft, implemented internally as "Dqlite" (Distributed SQLite). Dqlite enables SQLite to function as a replicated state machine across cluster nodes, providing fault tolerance and synchronous replication, effectively bridging the gap between SQLite's lightweight nature and the requirements of clustered state management.

MySQL and PostgreSQL, two fully featured relational database management systems (RDBMS), present a different storage paradigm emphasizing complex query capabilities, strong transactional consistency, and mature replication mechanisms. Integrating K3s with MySQL or PostgreSQL allows leveraging external database infrastructure common in enterprise setups. Both databases use a write-ahead log and MVCC (Multi-Version

71

Concurrency Control) to maintain consistency under concurrent operations, vital for ensuring the accuracy of desired-state records. The Kubernetes API server interacts with these databases through an etcd-compatible API layer, translating Kubernetes resource operations into consistent transactions. This setup is favored for larger clusters demanding high availability and horizontal scalability beyond what embedded solutions can provide. However, this convenience comes with added operational complexity and potential network latency between the K3s control plane and the database, necessitating careful configuration to optimize throughput and fault recovery times.

etcd, an open-source distributed key-value store designed explicitly for Kubernetes, is native to state synchronization and cluster membership coordination. It employs the Raft consensus algorithm to replicate data across nodes, providing strong consistency, fault tolerance, and high availability. K3s offers an embedded lightweight etcd variant called "Kine," which abstracts interactions between the Kubernetes API server and the actual storage backend by translating standard Kubernetes API calls into distributed transactions compatible with various databases. Kine enables K3s to support etcd semantics while allowing backend flexibility, including SQLite, MySQL, and PostgreSQL, consolidating the state storage model across deployment topologies. The etcd backend excels in multi-node, high fault-tolerance environments where consistent cluster state replication is critical. Its watch capability enables efficient event-driven synchronization, reducing the overhead of polling mechanisms.

K3s optimizes storage performance and reliability across deployment topologies by tailoring backend usage and replication strategies. In single-node or edge environments, embedded SQLite or Dqlite strikes an optimal balance by minimizing resource consumption and maintaining quick startup times. For high-availability clusters spanning multiple nodes, the adoption of external databases or etcd ensures data consistency despite node failures or network partitions. Replication factors and commit timeouts are fine-tuned to balance consistency guarantees and latency. Write-intensive operations benefit from batching and compaction strategies, reducing WAL file growth and I/O overhead. Additionally, persistent volume claims (PVCs) are configured to leverage fast storage media such as NVMe SSDs in cloud or bare-metal environments, enhancing disk throughput for backend writes.

Data consistency is enforced through transactional models inherent to each backend and augmented by Kubernetes' optimistic concurrency control mechanism utilizing resource versioning and preconditions for update operations. For instance, etcd guarantees linearizable reads and writes, enabling the API server to rely on strong consistency semantics. Conversely, the distributed SQLite implementation synchronizes leader election and log replication via Raft, preventing split-brain scenarios. MySQL and PostgreSQL clustering approaches, often involving synchronous or semi-synchronous replication, rely on external consensus to guarantee write durability before acknowledgment.

From a reliability standpoint, clustering ensures automatic failover, whereby in the event of a primary node failure, a replica assumes leadership with minimal disruption. Backup and restore processes integrate storage backend snapshots with Kubernetes custom resource definitions (CRDs), enabling point-in-time recovery. K3s further mitigates data loss risks by maintaining etcd defragmentation schedules and WAL pruning. Monitoring tools expose quantitative metrics such as commit latencies, replication lag, and disk utilization to facilitate proactive capacity planning.

The database storage subsystem in K3s is a layered architecture balancing lightweight embedded databases with advanced distributed storage systems, enabled by abstraction layers like Kine and Dqlite. This design allows K3s to flexibly adapt to diverse deployment requirements, ensuring consistent state synchronization, optimized performance, and fault-tolerant reliability across diverse cluster topologies. Understanding the trade-offs between SQLite, MySQL, PostgreSQL, and etcd is essential for designing resilient, scalable Kubernetes clusters tailored to specific operational contexts.

3.6. Image Management and Registry Configuration

K3s leverages `containerd` as its default container runtime, streamlining image management and registry interactions through a lightweight yet extensible architecture. Unlike more complex Kubernetes distributions bundled with multiple CRI implementations, K3s consolidates container lifecycle operations around `containerd`, enabling optimized image handling particularly suited for resource-constrained and edge environments.

Interaction with Container Registries via Containerd

`containerd` operates as the core component responsible for pulling, storing, and managing container images. K3s communicates directly with `containerd`'s API to orchestrate image lifecycle events, ensuring seamless integration with container registries. Upon scheduling pods, the K3s agent instructs `containerd` to retrieve the required container images from specified registries. This interaction relies on `containerd`'s configuration, which K3s manages primarily via a configuration file located at `/etc/rancher/k3s/registries.yaml`, allowing centralized control over registry endpoints, authentication credentials, and mirror specifications.

Configuring Private Registries

Accessing private registries necessitates customized credential and endpoint configurations. K3s supports this through a curated

74

registries.yaml file which conforms to containerd's registry mirror configuration schema, enabling:

- Specification of one or more mirrors per registry.

- Authentication secrets for registries requiring credentials (basic auth, tokens, or TLS client certificates).

- TLS verification configuration, allowing users to disable verification when necessary.

A typical registries.yaml example for a private registry appears as follows:

```
mirrors:
  "myprivateregistry.example.com":
    endpoint:
      - "https://myprivateregistry.example.com"
configs:
  "myprivateregistry.example.com":
    auth:
      username: myuser
      password: mypassword
    tls:
      insecure_skip_verify: true
```

Once deployed, K3s reloads containerd configurations dynamically, minimizing downtime and ensuring that pods referencing images hosted on private registries can authenticate and pull images successfully.

Image Caching Strategies

K3s optimizes image pull performance and network footprint through persistent local caching managed by containerd. Unlike standard Kubernetes, where image layers may be redundantly downloaded across nodes, K3s implements:

- Local image layer caching indexed by content-addressable identifiers (digest values).

- Efficient layer deduplication shared across multiple images.

- Proactive clean-up policies configurable via K3s arguments to control disk usage.

This caching mechanism reduces startup times for pods on repeated deployments and mitigates bandwidth constraints in edge settings. Administrators can configure cache retention policies using the `--image-cleanup` flag in the K3s daemon, balancing storage durability with resource constraints.

Deployment in Air-Gapped or Offline Environments

Operating K3s clusters without access to public container registries requires careful preparation of the image ecosystem. K3s facilitates air-gapped deployments through:

- **Pre-pulling and Exporting Images:** Images intended for deployment can be pulled onto a connected host, exported as tarballs via `ctr images export`, and subsequently imported into the offline cluster using `ctr images import`.

- **Local Registry Setup:** Deploying a private registry within the air-gapped network enables centralized image distribution without external exposure. K3s can then be pointed at this local registry through `registries.yaml`.

- **Static Image Bundles:** K3s supports static image lists specified in the configuration, which ensure essential system images are preloaded across nodes, reducing runtime image pulls.

The commands below illustrate image export and import using containerd's CLI:

```
# Export an image on a connected host
ctr images export alpine.tar docker.io/library/alpine:latest

# Transfer alpine.tar to offline K3s node and import
ctr images import alpine.tar
```

By harnessing such workflows, K3s maintains operational consistency and reliability despite disconnected network conditions.

K3s-Specific Optimizations in Image Management

K3s introduces several optimizations that enhance container image handling in resource-limited environments. These include:

- **Streamlined Containerd Configuration:** K3s simplifies `containerd` setup by embedding default registries and mirrors optimized for Rancher's ecosystem, reducing user configuration overhead.

- **Unified Binary and Reduced Dependencies:** The tightly integrated `k3s` binary bundles `containerd` and related tools, eliminating version mismatches and configuration drift often encountered in larger distributions.

- **Integrated Image Garbage Collection:** K3s employs a configurable image garbage collector that runs periodically to purge unused images, minimizing disk usage without manual intervention.

- **Lightweight Overlay Filesystem Support:** By default, K3s configures `containerd` to use overlayfs, which is more efficient in layered image storage and thus accelerates container startup times.

These enhancements enable faster bootstrapping, predictable disk utilization, and streamlined configuration management, particularly valuable in Kubernetes edge device scenarios with limited I/O and storage throughput.

Summary of Best Practices

For robust and performant image management in K3s deployments, several best practices emerge:

- Precisely configure `registries.yaml` to specify private or local registry endpoints, including proper authentication details to avoid image pull failures.

- Utilize image export/import commands for controlled propagation of images into air-gapped clusters, maintaining strict version control and network isolation.

- Enable and tune image cleanup features to balance resource usage with workload needs, especially in limited-storage environments.

- Prefer local registry mirrors proximate to cluster nodes to reduce latency and bandwidth demands.

- Leverage K3s's default optimizations, but review and customize `containerd` options when operating in unique environments requiring specialized network or storage considerations.

Through these mechanisms, K3s fosters efficient, reliable, and secure container image management tailored for modern Kubernetes use cases ranging from cloud-native to remote and constrained edge locations.

3.7. K3s Upgrades and Downgrades

K3s, a lightweight Kubernetes distribution optimized for resource-constrained environments, requires careful procedures and best practices when performing version changes in production clusters. Both upgrades and downgrades entail operational risks that must be mitigated to maintain cluster stability and application availability. The following outlines the recommended processes, common automation strategies, risk factors, rollback considerations, and the mechanisms K3s employs to minimize disruptions during version transitions.

Upgrade and Downgrade Procedures:

Version transitions in K3s typically involve replacing the existing K3s binary on all cluster nodes with the target version, followed by a controlled restart of cluster components. The process can be manual or automated but must preserve cluster data and ensure node compatibility. The procedure is generally sequenced as follows:

1. **Pre-upgrade planning:** Confirm compatibility between the current and target versions, review release notes for deprecated features, and identify any configuration changes required.

2. **Backup etcd and cluster state:** Create a snapshot of the cluster datastore if using the embedded etcd, as this state is critical for health restoration in case of failures.

3. **Drain worker nodes:** Safely evict running workloads from worker nodes by cordoning and draining them, minimizing disruption during node restarts.

4. **Upgrade control plane nodes:** Sequentially upgrade control plane nodes by updating the K3s binary, restarting the server processes, and verifying API server readiness.

5. **Upgrade worker nodes:** Once control plane nodes are stable, upgrade worker nodes similarly, resuming workload scheduling after validation.

6. **Post-upgrade validation:** Continuously monitor cluster health, pod status, and log files to detect latency spikes, API errors, or other anomalies.

Downgrades follow a similar path but incur higher risks due to potential incompatibilities. It is advisable to avoid downgrades unless absolutely necessary and with thorough validation against workload requirements and persistent storage schemas.

Best Practices for Safe Version Transitions:

- Incremental upgrades: Avoid skipping multiple versions; instead, upgrade through each minor version sequentially to reduce incompatibility and configuration drift.

- Blue-green or canary deployments: Utilize spare nodes or separate clusters to test new versions under real workloads before production-wide rollout.

- Automated backups: Integrate etcd snapshotting or external datastore backups into upgrade pipelines to enable fast rollback if needed.

- Readiness and liveness probes: Ensure probes are correctly configured to prevent traffic routing to unready pods during node restarts.

- Comprehensive monitoring: Employ metrics, alerting, and logging systems to track upgrade progress and detect regressions early.

- Configuration management: Store all K3s manifests, configurations, and custom resource definitions in version-controlled repositories to ease configuration reconciliation.

Automation Strategies:

Automation reduces human error and enforces repeatable, auditable upgrade and downgrade workflows. Common practices include:

- Declarative upgrade manifests: Using configuration management tools (e.g., Ansible, Terraform, or Helm) to declaratively specify K3s version and configuration state.

- Rolling updates with node selectors: Automating node filtering and sequential upgrades to limit impact scope.

- Pre- and post-upgrade checks: Embedding health checks, test suites, and policy enforcement gates into CI/CD pipelines that trigger upgrade sequences.

- Operator-driven management: Leveraging Kubernetes operators specialized in K3s lifecycle management to automate failover, backup, and rollback steps on upgrade failures.

An example script snippet automating an upgrade command on a K3s node appears below:

```bash
#!/bin/bash

TARGET_VERSION="v1.24.4+k3s1"

# Drain node to safely evict workloads
kubectl drain $(hostname) --ignore-daemonsets --delete-local-data

# Download and install the target K3s version
curl -sfL https://get.k3s.io | INSTALL_K3S_VERSION=
    $TARGET_VERSION sh -

# Uncordon node after upgrade
kubectl uncordon $(hostname)
```

Risks and Rollback Triggers:

Risks associated with K3s version transitions primarily include:

- API incompatibilities: Newer API versions may deprecate or remove APIs used by workloads or controllers.

- Data store schema changes: Etcd or embedded datastore schema updates may be irreversible or incompatible with previous versions.

- Node crash loops: Mismatched binaries and configurations can cause K3s agents or servers to fail repeatedly.

- Workload disruptions: Unplanned pod evictions or failed readiness probes result in service outages.

- Configuration drift: Changed cluster-level configurations can result in unexpected application behavior.

Common rollback triggers include:

- Persistent failure of control plane components to enter a Ready state.

- Workload pods stuck in CrashLoopBackOff after upgrade.

- Monitoring alerts indicating degraded cluster health or API latency errors.

- Failed backup restores or etcd election instability.

Minimizing Disruption During Migrations:

K3s incorporates several design decisions and features to reduce downtime and maintain cluster availability:

- Lightweight and modular architecture: Smaller binary size allows rapid upgrades and restarts, reducing downtime windows.

- Embedded datastore options: The built-in etcd or SQLite options enable faster snapshot backups and quicker recovery versus external datastores.

- Graceful node draining: Native integration with Kubernetes cordon and drain commands ensures workloads migrate smoothly away from upgrading nodes.

- Sequential and staggered upgrades: Encouraged upgrade approaches avoid full cluster downtime by upgrading control plane nodes one at a time and staggering worker upgrades.

- Version compatibility guarantees: K3s maintains strict se-
  mantic versioning policies to avoid breaking cluster state between minor versions.

- Health checks and probes awareness: K3s supports
  Kubernetes-native health checks extensively to prevent
  prematurely routing traffic to unavailable pods.

Ensuring comprehensive observability and disciplined operational
procedures is paramount. Combining these mechanisms with automation and robust rollback planning enables the safe rolling forward or backward of K3s versions, reducing risk exposure in production environments.

84

Chapter 4

Cluster Networking, Ingress, and Service Meshes

Behind every K3s deployment is an intricate web of communication, connectivity, and control. This chapter pulls back the curtain on the networking backbone, unpacks the realities of service discovery, and reveals how secure and scalable service-to-service communications come alive—even in constrained edge and hybrid environments.

4.1. Supported CNIs and Overlay Networks

K3s, as a lightweight Kubernetes distribution, provides support for multiple Container Network Interfaces (CNIs) that enable network connectivity between pods, nodes, and external networks. The choice of CNI profoundly impacts network performance, scalability, and resource consumption, particularly in environments with constrained computational or memory resources. This section examines the CNIs supported by K3s, focusing on the default solution, Flannel, as well as more advanced CNIs such as Calico and Cilium. It further analyzes the orchestration of overlay networks and the trade-offs involved in selecting an appropriate CNI for resource-limited contexts.

Flannel: The Default CNI in K3s

Flannel is the default CNI integrated into K3s, designed for simplicity and ease of use in lightweight cluster deployments. It operates primarily as a Layer 3 virtual network fabric, employing overlay networks to encapsulate pod-to-pod traffic over the underlying physical network. Flannel supports multiple backend mechanisms including VXLAN, host-gw, and IPsec, with VXLAN being the most common default.

The VXLAN backend creates a Layer 2 overlay network by encapsulating Ethernet frames within UDP packets, allowing pods on different hosts to communicate as if they were on the same subnet. This approach abstracts underlying network topologies and facilitates cross-host communication without complex routing configurations.

Advantages of Flannel include:

- **Simplicity**: Minimal configuration required, suitable for rapid cluster provisioning.

- **Lightweight Resource Usage**: Low CPU and memory overhead, aligning with the K3s philosophy.

- **Compatibility**: Works well across a wide range of network environments and kernel versions.

However, Flannel's simplicity comes with limitations:

- **Limited Network Policy Support**: Flannel does not natively enforce advanced policies, relying on higher layers or

86

external components.

- **Performance Overhead**: VXLAN encapsulation incurs extra packet processing and MTU fragmentation concerns.

- **Scalability Constraints**: Best suited for smaller clusters; large-scale deployments may expose limitations in routing efficiency and management.

Calico: Advanced Networking with Policy Enforcement

Calico provides an alternative CNI option offering a rich feature set focused on high performance, scalability, and fine-grained network security. Unlike Flannel's overlay networks, Calico primarily implements a Layer 3 routing model, leveraging Border Gateway Protocol (BGP) or IP-in-IP encapsulation to distribute routing information.

Calico operates by assigning each pod an IP address from a routable IP pool, integrating directly with the underlying network infrastructure. Nodes exchange route information via BGP, enabling direct packet forwarding between hosts without encapsulation when supported by the network environment. When encapsulation is necessary, IP-in-IP or VXLAN modes can be selected.

Key capabilities include:

- **Network Policy Enforcement**: Implements Kubernetes NetworkPolicies with granular control over ingress and egress traffic.

- **Optimized Performance**: Native Layer 3 routing reduces encapsulation overhead, improving throughput and reducing latency.

- **Scalability**: Suitable for extensive, multi-tenant clusters due to efficient routing and policy mechanisms.

Nonetheless, Calico requires more intricate configuration and operational knowledge, including BGP peering setup in certain modes. Its resource footprint is modest but higher than Flannel, warranting consideration in highly constrained environments.

Cilium: Leveraging eBPF for Network and Security

Cilium embodies a modern approach to container networking by utilizing Linux's extended Berkeley Packet Filter (eBPF) technology. eBPF enables programmable kernel-level packet processing, allowing Cilium to implement network routing, security enforcement, and load balancing with high efficiency and flexibility.

Cilium supports overlay networking with VXLAN and supports a novel, more efficient datapath through Direct Server Return (DSR) and Transparent Encryption. It also integrates deeply with Kubernetes mechanisms to enforce identity-based network policies that operate at both Layer 3/4 and Layer 7.

Distinctive features include:

- **High-Performance Packet Processing**: eBPF allows offloading complex logic to the kernel, reducing context switches and improving throughput.

- **Extended Security Model**: Supports fine-grained network security policies, application-awareness, and integration with service mesh frameworks.

- **Rich Observability**: Provides detailed telemetry and troubleshooting tools for network flows.

The complexity and resource implications of Cilium are higher than Flannel or Calico. Moreover, its reliance on recent Linux kernel features requires compatibility checks in the deployment environment.

Overlay Network Orchestration and Trade-offs

Overlay networks encapsulate pod network traffic to enable communication over diverse or non-uniform physical infrastructures. They abstract away network heterogeneity and facilitate pod mobility across hosts. The orchestration of overlay networks involves automatic management of encapsulation keys, IP address allocations, and route propagation.

Trade-offs in selecting and orchestrating overlay networks center around performance, complexity, and resource consumption:

- **Performance vs. Simplicity**: Overlay encapsulation adds CPU overhead and increases latency relative to direct routing models but simplifies cross-host communication.

- **Security vs. Resource Usage**: Advanced policy enforcement (e.g., with Calico or Cilium) improves security but often increases CPU and memory requirements.

- **Scalability vs. Operational Complexity**: More sophisticated CNIs enable scaling to larger clusters with complex policies but demand thorough operational expertise.

Considerations for Resource-Limited Environments

In resource-constrained deployments, such as edge computing nodes or small IoT clusters, careful CNI selection is critical. The minimalism of Flannel aligns well with hardware limitations, offering satisfactory pod networking capabilities with minimal overhead. Its trade-off involves limited security at the network layer, which may necessitate alternative security measures.

Calico can be used in these environments if resources permit, especially when network policy enforcement is essential. Its deployment can be optimized by disabling advanced features unnecessary for the use case.

Cilium, while powerful, generally requires more recent kernels and greater resource availability. It is best suited for environments where advanced security, observability, and layered network policies justify its overhead.

Ultimately, operators must balance the network performance needs, security requirements, and operational overhead against hardware and workload constraints. Hybrid approaches mixing lightweight CNIs with external security controls or selective use of advanced features may offer optimal trade-offs in heterogeneous infrastructures.

The selection and orchestration of CNIs in K3s thus constitutes a foundational decision shaping cluster networking behavior, impacting performance, security, and manageability in production and constrained environments alike.

4.2. Service Discovery and DNS Internals

Service discovery within Kubernetes is a foundational capability that enables seamless inter-component communication and dynamic scaling of workloads. In lightweight Kubernetes distributions such as K3s, internal service discovery leans heavily on implementation choices tailored to edge environments-most notably, the use of CoreDNS as the default DNS server. The mechanisms by which CoreDNS is configured and managed in K3s, combined with the unique constraints found in edge clusters, expose important considerations and best practices in service naming, customization, and resilience.

CoreDNS operates as a flexible, plugin-based DNS server that serves the cluster's internal DNS queries. In K3s, CoreDNS is deployed as a DaemonSet, ensuring that DNS resolution is consistently available on every node. This is critical for edge clusters that may have intermittent network conditions or limited resources. The CoreDNS pods run within the kube-system namespace and listen on UDP and TCP port 53, intercepting DNS queries originating from pods via the node-local kubelet-configured DNS stub domain. This design enhances resilience and reduces latency by localizing DNS resolution.

The CoreDNS configuration is managed through a ConfigMap named `coredns` in the `kube-system` namespace. This ConfigMap uses a Corefile syntax that defines how queries to various domains are processed. A typical Corefile configuration in K3s includes a set of default plugins such as `kubernetes`, `prometheus`, `forward`, and `cache`. The `kubernetes` plugin is crucial; it integrates directly with Kubernetes API server endpoints to watch for changes in services, pods, and endpoints, enabling automatic updates to DNS mappings.

A minimal example of an internal cluster Corefile segment looks as follows:

```
.:53 {
    errors
    health
    kubernetes cluster.local in-addr.arpa ip6.arpa {
       pods insecure
       fallthrough in-addr.arpa ip6.arpa
       ttl 30
    }
    prometheus :9153
    forward . /etc/resolv.conf
    cache 30
    loop
    reload
    loadbalance
}
```

Here, the `kubernetes` plugin intercepts queries for services within the `cluster.local` domain and directs them to the relevant service IPs and pod IPs, while `forward` passes non-cluster queries to upstream DNS servers defined in `/etc/resolv.conf`. The `cache` plugin improves DNS response time by caching results, and `loadbalance` prevents hotspotting of backends.

Edge clusters impose additional challenges on CoreDNS configurations. Due to the variability of network connectivity and constrained compute resources in edge nodes, DNS servers must be highly available and lightweight. Deploying CoreDNS as a DaemonSet helps provide local DNS resolution even if connectivity to the master node fluctuates. Additionally, given that edge environments may not have reliable or consistent external DNS, the forward plugin configuration often requires custom upstream resolvers or fallback mechanisms to ensure resolution continuity.

In some edge scenarios, service discovery needs extend beyond the standard cluster.local namespace. K3s facilitates custom DNS setups by allowing multiple DNS domains or rewrites via CoreDNS plugins such as rewrite or hosts. For instance, implementing custom domain suffixes for specific applications or environments can minimize conflict and improve discoverability. Consider the following addition to a Corefile for explicit domain rewriting:

```
rewrite name svc.external.local svc.cluster.local
```

This instructs CoreDNS to map queries for svc.external.local to the internal svc.cluster.local namespace, which can be leveraged for edge services that coexist with external service mesh components or hybrid clusters.

Best practices for naming conventions and resilience in CoreDNS are essential for maintaining stable service discovery across diverse edge deployments. Consistent and hierarchical naming schemes, such as {service}.{namespace}.svc.cluster.local, are vital for conflict avoidance and intuitiveness. Services should be named avoiding overly generic identifiers, especially when clusters are federated or communicate externally.

Resilience is addressed by controlling CoreDNS query timeouts and retries through plugin configurations to handle transient network issues common in edge environments. The loop plugin, for example, prevents infinite recursion in DNS queries that may occur due to misconfiguration. Load balancing and caching plugin parameters must be tuned to balance response speed against resource consumption.

In addition to CoreDNS configuration, K3s integrates tightly with node-local DNS caching mechanisms to optimize DNS resolution latency and reduce external query load. A node-local DNS cache, often deployed as a DaemonSet alongside CoreDNS, intercepts pod DNS requests at the node level, reducing cross-node query traffic and failure domains. This architecture is particularly advantageous at the edge, where minimizing network chatter and balancing resource use are priorities.

Service discovery within K3s edge clusters hinges on the effective deployment and customization of CoreDNS. Its plugin model allows detailed control over DNS forwarding, rewriting, caching, and health checks, which are indispensable for tailored edge scenarios. Emphasizing robust naming conventions and deploying node-local caches further contribute to resilient, performant internal DNS resolution that underpins reliable service-to-service communication in constrained and unpredictable edge environments.

4.3. Ingress Controller Deployments

Ingress controllers serve as the gatekeepers for external traffic entering Kubernetes clusters, managing routing, load balancing, and security policies for inbound requests. Within lightweight Kubernetes distributions such as K3s, integrating ingress controllers like Traefik, NGINX, or bespoke implementations requires precise configuration to ensure robust and secure traffic flow, especially when exposed to untrusted networks. This section elaborates on deployment strategies, ingress resource configurations, TLS termination approaches, and best practices for managing ingress within K3s environments.

K3s, by default, includes Traefik as its built-in ingress controller, optimized for resource efficiency while providing essential ingress functionality. However, users often replace or complement Traefik with NGINX or custom ingress controllers to better suit specific traffic management needs or compliance requirements. Deploying an ingress controller starts with selecting the appropriate controller and then installing it within the cluster namespace, ensuring it has the necessary cluster role bindings and service accounts to manage ingress resources.

For example, deploying the NGINX ingress controller in K3s involves the following command sequence, kubectl being the common interface for Kubernetes API interactions:

```
kubectl apply -f https://raw.githubusercontent.com/kubernetes/
    ingress-nginx/controller-v1.8.1/deploy/static/provider/k3s/
    deploy.yaml
```

This installs the controller with default configurations optimized for K3s, including a load balancer service for external traffic ingress. Custom ingress controllers follow a similar paradigm, with manifests tailored to the specific controller's requirements and integration points.

Ingress resources define routing rules that link external HTTP and HTTPS requests to internal services based on hostnames and paths. A typical ingress resource manifests as follows:

```
apiVersion: networking.k8s.io/v1
kind: Ingress
metadata:
  name: example-ingress
  annotations:
    nginx.ingress.kubernetes.io/rewrite-target: /
spec:
  ingressClassName: nginx
  rules:
  - host: www.example.com
    http:
      paths:
      - path: /app1
        pathType: Prefix
        backend:
          service:
            name: app1-service
            port:
              number: 80
```

```
tls:
- hosts:
  - www.example.com
  secretName: example-tls-secret
```

Key elements include the `ingressClassName` field directing the resource to the intended ingress controller, the host and path rules for request routing, and a TLS section specifying termination settings via Kubernetes secrets holding certificate data.

TLS termination within ingress is pivotal for securing traffic from untrusted networks. It can be implemented on the ingress controller itself, acting as a TLS terminator and offloading the encryption and decryption overhead from backend services. Certificates, often managed by cert-manager or equivalent tooling, reside in Kubernetes secrets referenced in the ingress resource's `tls` section. This design enables encrypted communication between clients and the ingress controller while allowing backend services to receive plain HTTP traffic internally, simplifying service configuration.

When managing ingress in environments exposed to untrusted networks, several strategies enhance security and resilience:

- **Whitelist IP Ranges:** Annotations or ingress controller configurations can restrict access by IP, allowing only trusted clients to reach sensitive applications.

- **Mutual TLS (mTLS):** Though more complex, configuring mTLS between clients and ingress controllers adds a layer of authentication.

- **Rate Limiting and Request Filtering:** Controllers like NGINX provide annotations to limit request rates, mitigate brute-force attacks, and filter malicious patterns.

- **Network Policies and Firewalling:** K3s complements ingress security with network policies controlling pod-level communication and firewall rules governing cluster ingress points.

Integration of custom ingress controllers often stems from specific operational requirements or when existing controllers lack desired features. Custom controllers must implement the Kubernetes ingress controller interface, watch ingress resource changes, and update their routing configurations accordingly. With K3s's lightweight footprint, it is vital to monitor resource consumption and performance when deploying feature-rich or customized ingress controllers.

For automated certificate management in ingress controllers, cert-manager is the de facto solution in Kubernetes ecosystems. It automates the issuance and renewal of TLS certificates from ACME-compatible certificate authorities, including Let's Encrypt. The workflow consists of creating `Certificate` and `Issuer` resources, which the cert-manager controller watches to provision and refresh secrets consumed by ingress resources for TLS termination.

Ingress controllers output metrics and logs critical for production deployments. Centralized logging and monitoring solutions should be configured to capture ingress activity, TLS handshake failures, request latencies, and error rates. These insights allow fine-tuning of ingress configurations, capacity planning, and early detection of security incidents.

Effective ingress controller deployment in K3s involves selecting or customizing an ingress controller that fits operational constraints, defining ingress resources with precise routing and security policies, implementing TLS termination aligned to external threats, and deploying ancillary security measures to mitigate exposure from untrusted networks. Mastery of ingress configurations and management underpins reliable and secure service exposure in lightweight Kubernetes environments.

4.4. ServiceLB and External Load Balancer Integration

The `ServiceLB` component in K3s serves as a lightweight built-in load balancer designed to provide basic ingress capabilities within the cluster without requiring more complex or resource-intensive solutions. It enables service exposure and traffic distribution among pods via the well-known `LoadBalancer` type in Kubernetes services, but with a minimalist footprint suitable for edge, resource-constrained environments, and development use cases.

At its core, `ServiceLB` implements load balancing by managing IP address allocations within the cluster and routing external service traffic directly to cluster nodes through IPVS (IP Virtual Server) or simpler iptables-based proxying. Unlike cloud-native load balancers that benefit from provider APIs and native infrastructure, `ServiceLB` abstracts a bare-metal or local network environment by assigning virtual IPs (VIPs) that map to the service endpoints managed by K3s. As a result, it offers a seamless experience for users wanting to expose services without additional configuration or dependencies beyond K3s itself.

The load balancing mechanism inside `ServiceLB` relies on the Kubernetes Service abstraction, where each `LoadBalancer` service is allocated a stable virtual IP address. This IP is then advertised to cluster nodes and clients within the same network. Incoming traffic to the VIP is distributed by IPVS to backend pod endpoints based on configured balancing algorithms, typically round-robin or least connections, depending on system support and implementation. This design ensures scalability and fault tolerance at the service level, while retaining simplicity.

```
kubectl apply -f - <<EOF
apiVersion: v1
kind: Service
metadata:
  name: example-service-lb
spec:
```

```
type: LoadBalancer
selector:
  app: example-app
ports:
- port: 80
  targetPort: 8080
EOF
```

The above manifest shows the minimal configuration for exposing an application using `ServiceLB` in K3s. After deployment, a virtual IP will be assigned to `example-service-lb`, enabling external access.

While `ServiceLB` is sufficient for basic scenarios, its limitations become evident in more advanced networking contexts, such as multi-node clustering across different L2 networks, high availability under node failures, and external accessibility through public internet gateways. To enhance these capabilities, K3s integrates smoothly with external load balancers, depending on the target environment: MetalLB for bare-metal or private clusters, and cloud provider-specific load balancers in public or hybrid cloud deployments.

MetalLB is an open-source load balancer implementation tailored for Kubernetes clusters that run in environments lacking native load balancing. It extends the concept of announcing virtual IPs by leveraging protocols like BGP (Border Gateway Protocol) or ARP (Address Resolution Protocol) to advertise service VIPs to the local network or upstream routers. When integrated into K3s, MetalLB replaces or complements the internal `ServiceLB` by providing more robust, scalable IP address management and high-availability properties.

MetalLB operates in two modes: Layer 2 mode, which relies on ARP to announce VIPs on the local subnet, suitable for simple flat network topologies; and BGP mode, which peers with network routers to propagate VIP routes across more complex network fabrics. This flexibility enables K3s clusters employing MetalLB to effectively bridge internal cluster service endpoints to physical or virtual networks beyond the cluster boundary.

Integrating MetalLB into K3s involves deploying its control plane components as standard Kubernetes manifests, configuring IP address pools that define the range of external VIPs allocatable to LoadBalancer services, and ensuring network infrastructure compatibility with the chosen announcement protocol. This setup provides external clients, whether within a corporate network or directly on the internet perimeter, with transparent access to services hosted in K3s, preserving rich load balancing semantics.

Example MetalLB configuration in K3s:

```
apiVersion: metallb.io/v1beta1
kind: IPAddressPool
metadata:
  name: k3s-lb-pool
  namespace: metallb-system
spec:
  addresses:
  - 192.168.1.240-192.168.1.250
---
apiVersion: metallb.io/v1beta1
kind: L2Advertisement
metadata:
  name: l2-advertisement
  namespace: metallb-system
spec:
  ipAddressPools:
  - k3s-lb-pool
```

Cloud providers such as AWS, Azure, GCP, and others provide fully managed load balancers tightly integrated with their infrastructure, supporting advanced features such as global routing, autoscaling, security policies, and native TLS termination. When deploying K3s within public clouds or hybrid cloud architectures, the Kubernetes service type LoadBalancer automatically triggers the provisioning of such external load balancers via the cloud provider's controller manager.

K3s incorporates lightweight cloud controller managers and service controllers that enable out-of-the-box provisioning of cloud-native load balancers according to the Kubernetes Service configurations. This seamless integration eliminates manual IP management and allows K3s clusters to leverage high availability, performance, and resilience features of cloud load balancing - crucial for production-grade deployments at scale.

Bridging internal K3s cluster networks to public clouds or hybrid environments involves overcoming challenges such as disparate network topologies, private IP address spaces, and firewall policies. Common techniques include:

- Network Address Translation (NAT) and port forwarding to expose cluster services on public interfaces while preserving backend pod routing.

- VPN tunnels or overlay networks (e.g., WireGuard, Calico) to interconnect disparate network segments securely.

- Cloud egress gateways or ingress controllers deployed within K3s to act as protocol-aware proxies or reverse proxies.

- DNS-based service discovery combined with external load balancer endpoints to route traffic dynamically.

These mechanisms allow K3s clusters to remain network agnostic internally while interoperating fluidly with external infrastructure, enabling scalable and secure multi-environment service delivery.

ServiceLB offers an accessible entry point into load balancing for K3s clusters, especially in edge or local development contexts. For production-ready, scalable external load balancing, MetalLB provides critical enhancements in bare-metal or private data centers, while cloud provider native load balancers offer seamless integration within public cloud platforms. Bridging K3s clustering to external networks leverages a combination of IP management, protocol announcements, and hybrid networking paradigms - forming the foundation for resilient, accessible Kubernetes service delivery across diverse deployment environments.

4.5. Advanced Network Policy Management

Network policies serve as a critical component in securing intra-cluster communication by defining rules that regulate traffic flow between pods, namespaces, and external endpoints. Their role becomes significantly amplified in multi-tenant environments where resource isolation and security boundaries must be rigorously enforced to prevent lateral movement and unauthorized data access.

At the core, a network policy is a set of directives interpreted by the network plugin to allow or deny traffic based on pod selectors, namespaces, ports, and protocols. This declarative specification directly influences the underlying networking fabric, delivering fine-grained control over how workloads interact within a cluster. The enforcement of these policies ensures that only explicitly permitted traffic traverses, reducing the attack surface.

Consider a multi-tenant Kubernetes cluster supporting several teams or projects, each encapsulated in its own namespace. From a security standpoint, it is paramount to isolate tenants not merely at the namespace level but also at network boundaries. This reduces the risk of accidental or malicious cross-tenant communication. For instance, network policies can prevent pods in one namespace from establishing connections to pods in another unless explicitly allowed.

A typical pattern involves implementing default-deny ingress and egress policies, creating a zero-trust framework where no pod may send or receive traffic unless authorized. This strategy starts with a catch-all rule denying all traffic:

```
apiVersion: networking.k8s.io/v1
kind: NetworkPolicy
metadata:
  name: default-deny-all
  namespace: <namespace>
spec:
  podSelector: {}
  policyTypes:
  - Ingress
```

```
- Egress
ingress: []
egress: []
```

By applying this to each tenant namespace, one establishes stringent baseline controls. Afterward, selective ingress and egress
rules open specific communication paths. For instance, allowing frontend pods to connect to backend services within the same
namespace utilizes podSelector-based rules with port and protocol
restrictions:

```
apiVersion: networking.k8s.io/v1
kind: NetworkPolicy
metadata:
  name: allow-frontend-to-backend
  namespace: tenant-a
spec:
  podSelector:
    matchLabels:
      role: backend
  policyTypes:
  - Ingress
  ingress:
  - from:
    - podSelector:
        matchLabels:
          role: frontend
    ports:
    - protocol: TCP
      port: 8080
```

This explicit allowance ensures that only frontend pods initiate
connections to backend pods on port 8080, blocking any other
sources or ports.

Robust security boundaries further require inter-namespace isolation. To enforce this, network policies can leverage namespace selectors. For example, preventing all ingress traffic from
other namespaces except those labeled for a trusted shared service
namespace:

```
apiVersion: networking.k8s.io/v1
kind: NetworkPolicy
metadata:
  name: restrict-external-namespace-ingress
  namespace: tenant-b
```

```
spec:
  podSelector: {}
  policyTypes:
  - Ingress
  ingress:
  - from:
    - namespaceSelector:
        matchLabels:
          name: shared-services
```

This design maintains strict intra-tenant communication while permitting essential interactions with shared infrastructure components such as monitoring or logging agents.

The complexity increases when handling multi-tenant overlapping IP spaces or encrypted traffic. Advanced network policy implementations may integrate with service meshes or Layer 7 proxies to extend policy enforcement beyond IP addresses and ports, allowing identity- and attribute-based access control. For example, Istio's Authorization Policy offers fine-grained control at the HTTP/messaging protocol level, complementing traditional network policies with application-layer security.

Enforcement mechanisms depend heavily on the chosen CNI (Container Network Interface) plugin. Some plugins, like Calico or Cilium, provide enhanced policy capabilities, including support for eBPF-based enforcement, scalable rule evaluation, and integration with Kubernetes labels and annotations. These advanced features enable efficient policy updates, dynamic adaptation to pod lifecycle events, and granular visibility into policy enforcement status.

Monitoring the effects of network policies is critical to ensure their correctness and to troubleshoot unintended blockages. Tools such as kubectl commands, CNI-specific diagnostics, and network visualization utilities help verify connectivity and policy compliance. For example, Calico provides detailed logs and metrics for denied connections, facilitating proactive policy tuning.

Advanced network policy management requires a disciplined approach anchored in default-deny principles, precise pod- and namespace-level selectors, and layered security boundaries that reflect tenant isolation goals. Leveraging the capabilities of modern CNIs and integrating application-layer enforcement mechanisms ensures resilient and adaptable control of intra-cluster traffic, a cornerstone for securing multi-tenant Kubernetes environments.

4.6. Service Mesh Architectures on K3s

The deployment of service meshes on lightweight Kubernetes distributions such as K3s presents a distinctive set of architectural and operational considerations. K3s, designed explicitly for resource-constrained environments and edge computing, differs fundamentally from full-scale Kubernetes clusters in terms of resource availability, node capabilities, and network topology. Consequently, running full-featured service meshes-like Istio-as well as lightweight alternatives such as Linkerd requires careful adaptation of traditional architectures and operational patterns to fit within these constraints.

A primary technical challenge arises in the sidecar injection model, which is central to most service meshes. In typical Kubernetes clusters, automatic sidecar injection is configured via mutating admission webhooks, enabling seamless insertion of proxy containers alongside workloads. K3s supports these webhooks, but due to its minimalist design and reduced control plane footprint, webhook scalability and reliability can be impacted, especially on clusters with limited CPU and memory resources. Moreover, edge nodes often impose strict limits on pod density and memory consumption per node, which necessitates judicious tuning or selective sidecar deployment to avoid exhaustion of available resources.

With Istio on K3s, the sidecar Envoy proxy, robust and feature-rich, can consume upwards of 50 to 100 MB of memory per instance, depending on configuration. When multiplied across multiple pods on a resource-limited node, this overhead may overwhelm node capabilities. To mitigate this, configurations commonly restrict sidecar injection to critical workloads only, or employ Istio's Sidecar resource to limit the sidecar's visibility to a subset of services, thereby optimizing memory and CPU usage. Additionally, Istio's control plane components-such as Pilot, Citadel, and Galley-have nontrivial resource requirements. Lightweight profiles, partial component deployments, or offloading control plane functions to external clusters are strategies frequently employed to maintain a functional mesh without overburdening the cluster.

Linkerd, by contrast, is architected with a lightweight and minimalist design philosophy, leading to significantly lower per-proxy resource consumption. Its proxy is implemented in Rust, focusing on speed and minimal memory footprint, often consuming roughly 10–20 MB per sidecar pod. This characteristic makes Linkerd naturally more amenable to edge and small-cluster environments such as those orchestrated by K3s. Further, Linkerd's control plane components are smaller and less complex, enabling deployments on single nodes without substantial performance trade-offs. Mesh management operations, including telemetry collection and certificate rotations, impose a lighter operational burden. This smaller resource footprint facilitates simpler mesh scaling and fault tolerance under constrained conditions.

Despite the lean design advantages of Linkerd, several operational patterns remain critical across both service meshes on K3s installations. These patterns include:

- Enabling sidecar injection only for selected namespaces or deployments where observability or traffic management is required, rather than enabling injection cluster-wide by default. This selective approach avoids unnecessary resource consumption and reduces the attack surface.

- Applying tailored resource quotas and limits for mesh components and injected proxies to prevent resource contention with application containers.

- Employing refined pod affinity and anti-affinity rules to distribute mesh control plane components effectively while considering the limited capacity of edge nodes.

An intrinsic challenge is multi-cluster or multi-edge mesh federation extending across multiple K3s clusters. Due to K3s's simplicity, mesh control planes often require architectural abstraction, such as off-cluster control planes or external service registries. Hybrid architectures utilize centralized mesh control planes that interface with multiple K3s data planes at the edge, balancing control and observability with local autonomy and resilience. This also enables consolidated telemetry and policy management, reducing complexity and resource load on each edge cluster.

Continuous mesh management in K3s environments is complicated by intermittent network connectivity and transient node availability, common in edge scenarios. Thus, service meshes deployed on K3s favor designs supporting eventual consistency in configuration and policy enforcement, tolerating temporary inconsistencies in routing or telemetry reporting. Workload health telemetry can be locally cached and synchronized opportunistically to improve resilience. Additionally, the use of simplified security models or scopes for mTLS and authorization policies reduces complexity, ensuring minimal latency and overhead.

Resource consumption profiling and monitoring tools tailored for lightweight clusters provide essential feedback loops for mesh tuning on K3s. Organizations often implement enhanced observability at the edge with integrated logging and metrics pipelines optimized for low bandwidth and intermittent connectivity. Aggregating telemetry in a hierarchical manner, with edge clusters emitting summarized data upstream, minimizes the overhead of full-fidelity data streaming.

The deployment of service mesh architectures on K3s involves bal-

106

ancing the feature-rich capabilities of full meshes such as Istio with the resource-conscious efficiency of lightweight options like Linkerd. Key design and operational patterns-selective sidecar injection, resource constraint enforcement, architectural federation, and resilience-aware management-ensure that mesh benefits are realized without compromising the intrinsic constraints of edge-focused Kubernetes environments.

4.7. Securing Cluster Communications

Effective security of cluster communications hinges on ensuring confidentiality, integrity, and authenticity of data both in transit and at rest. These requirements drive the adoption of cryptographic methods, network overlay architectures, and trust models tailored to safeguard internal and external communication channels. This section elucidates methodologies for encrypting data flows, constructing VPN overlays to encapsulate traffic, and implementing zero trust networking principles that minimize implicit trust within cluster environments.

Encryption of Data in Transit and at Rest

Data in transit within clusters-including control plane messages, distributed workflow data, and state synchronization-must be protected against eavesdropping, man-in-the-middle (MITM) attacks, and replay attempts. The predominant mechanism for protecting such communication is Transport Layer Security (TLS), which provides confidentiality and message integrity through symmetric encryption algorithms combined with asymmetric key exchanges for session key establishment.

For internal cluster communication, mutual TLS (mTLS) is commonly employed to enforce bidirectional authentication. Each node possesses a unique certificate signed by an internal certificate authority (CA). This ensures only authorized endpoints communicate, and any intrusion attempts are detected early. The TLS handshake mandates verification of certificates, thwarting unauthorized nodes from injecting or intercepting packets.

Data at rest within the cluster-such as logs, databases, and persistent storage volumes-must also be encrypted to prevent offline data theft, especially in multi-tenant environments. Disk encryption using technologies like LUKS, encrypted file systems such as eCryptfs or ZFS native encryption, and application-level encryption of sensitive fields constitute layered security. The choice between full disk encryption versus file-level encryption depends on performance overhead, granularity of control, and key management capabilities.

Key management is critical. Centralized vault services like HashiCorp Vault enable dynamic secret provisioning, automated certificate renewal, and hardware security module (HSM) integration to safeguard cryptographic credentials. Access control policies must enforce least privilege principles and rotate keys periodically to reduce exposure.

Building VPN Overlays for Secure Encapsulation

Virtual Private Network (VPN) overlays create encrypted tunnels over existing untrusted networks, logically isolating cluster communication paths. Unlike traditional flat networks, overlay networks encapsulate packets using tunneling protocols that add payload encryption and integrity checks.

WireGuard, IPSec, and OpenVPN are popular technologies for building these overlays. WireGuard, in particular, offers a lightweight codebase with modern cryptography (Noise protocol framework) and minimal configuration complexity. The interface establishes point-to-point tunnels between cluster nodes, employing Curve25519 for key exchange and ChaCha20-Poly1305 for symmetric encryption.

An exemplary WireGuard configuration involves each node maintaining a private and public key pair. Individual endpoint IP addresses within the overlay are assigned non-conflicting subnets. Routing tables on each node direct cluster-bound traffic through the WireGuard interface:

```
[Interface]
PrivateKey = <node-private-key>
Address = 10.0.0.1/24

[Peer]
PublicKey = <peer1-public-key>
AllowedIPs = 10.0.0.2/32
Endpoint = peer1.example.com:51820

[Peer]
PublicKey = <peer2-public-key>
AllowedIPs = 10.0.0.3/32
Endpoint = peer2.example.com:51820
```

The overlay network encrypts all packets traversing public or untrusted infrastructure. Additionally, route-based segmentation models can isolate distinct cluster zones, where overlay subnets are mapped to logical roles, such as management, storage replication, or application tiers.

Overlay VPNs complement traditional perimeter security by enabling cryptographically enforced segmentation and minimizing exposure of internal IP addresses. These tunnels provide end-to-end confidentiality and resistance against traffic analysis when paired with padding or obfuscation techniques.

Zero Trust Networking Principles in Cluster Environments

Zero trust networking (ZTN) represents a paradigm shift from perimeter-based defenses to continuous verification and granular policy enforcement. In the context of cluster communications, ZTN assumes no implicit trust between nodes irrespective of their network location or prior authentication.

Implementing zero trust involves several components:

- **Strong Identity and Authentication:** Every request is authenticated and authorized before granting resource access. Utilizing hardware-backed identities (e.g., TPM or secure enclave attestation) strengthens trust assertions beyond software credentials.

- **Microsegmentation:** Networks are segmented into isolated pods, each governed by explicit, least-privilege policies enforced via firewalls or software-defined networking (SDN). East-west traffic within clusters is filtered strictly to permitted flows.

- **Continuous Monitoring and Anomaly Detection:** Traffic patterns are analyzed in real-time to detect deviations from normal behavior, allowing rapid incident response to lateral movement or data exfiltration attempts.

- **Policy-Driven Access Controls:** Role-based access control (RBAC) or attribute-based access control (ABAC) systems define permissions dynamically based on identity, device posture, geographic location, and time constraints.

Service meshes such as Istio or Linkerd exemplify practical zero trust enforcement by providing transparent mTLS encryption between service endpoints, dynamic policy injection, and telemetry aggregation. Integration with identity providers and certificate issuance automates secure mutual authentication, eliminating manual key distribution.

For outbound cluster communications, ZTN principles dictate gateway proxies with enforced egress policies, mandatory multifactor authentication, and session auditing. These controls prevent compromised internal nodes from acting maliciously or leaking sensitive information.

Integrated Security Recipes for Comprehensive Protection

Combining encryption, VPN overlays, and zero trust best practices yields a defense-in-depth architecture. A practical recipe for securing cluster communications includes:

- Enable mTLS for all internal APIs and inter-node communication. Employ automatic certificate rotation via an internal PKI.

- Deploy a WireGuard-based VPN overlay spanning all cluster nodes to encrypt traffic traversing public or hybrid cloud infrastructure, with route isolation per functional domain.

- Establish microsegmentation using SDN controllers or service meshes to enforce granular traffic policies.

- Implement continuous authentication with ephemeral credentials tied to device attestation or identity federation.

- Use centralized secret management platforms for encryption keys, API tokens, and certificates, integrating audit logs for compliance.

- Monitor cluster telemetry continuously, raising alerts on anomalous communication patterns or policy violations.

```
Example: Encrypted cluster communication flow
  Client Node --> WireGuard Tunnel --> mTLS-secured Service Mesh Proxy --> De
stination Service

  Each layer encrypts and authenticates traffic independently, ensuring
  confidentiality and integrity even if a single layer is compromised.
```

These combined mechanisms create a resilient and transparent security fabric that simultaneously supports performance-sensitive workloads while adhering to rigorous protection mandates. By embedding encryption and zero trust principles deeply into cluster architectures, organizations mitigate attack surfaces, reduce insider threat risks, and establish trustworthy multi-tenant operations.

The interplay between overlay network designs and cryptographic trust models fosters scalable security without sacrificing operational agility. Continuous refinement of policies and cryptographic algorithms ensures adaptation to evolving threat landscapes and advances in quantum-resistant technologies.

Chapter 5

Storage Architecture and Data Management

Storage in distributed systems is often misunderstood—and in lightweight environments, it's even more critical to get it right. This chapter uncovers the principles and practicalities behind K3s's data storage, persistence, and backup strategies, ensuring your clusters are resilient, secure, and ready for anything the edge can throw at them.

5.1. Ephemeral vs. Persistent Data in K3s

Within Kubernetes distributions such as K3s, an understanding of data persistence is fundamental for ensuring the reliability and durability of applications. Data managed by containerized workloads generally falls into two categories: *ephemeral* and *persistent*. Each category entails distinct characteristics, lifecycle expectations, and implications for cluster architecture and storage strategy.

Ephemeral data refers to transient data generated and consumed during the lifetime of a pod or container, without the expectation of longevity beyond that scope. Typical examples include:

- **Local scratch space**: Temporary files written during batch processing, intermediary computation artifacts, or caches that accelerate runtime performance.

- **Pod logs**: Diagnostic logs stored locally before being shipped to centralized logging services.

- **In-memory caches and session states**: Short-lived data structures confined within container memory or local ephemeral storage.

In K3s, ephemeral storage commonly leverages the node's host filesystem, typically mounted into the pod through the `emptyDir` volume type. This volume is created when a pod is assigned to a node and destroyed upon pod termination, closely coupling the data lifecycle with the pod lifecycle. Importantly, such data does not survive pod rescheduling or node failures.

The ephemeral nature of this data dictates the following design considerations:

- **Performance prioritization**: Local ephemeral volumes provide the lowest latency and highest throughput since they avoid network overhead.

- **Cost economy**: Avoids complexity and expense of persistent storage systems for data where persistence is nonessential.

- **High volatility tolerance**: Workloads that can tolerate data loss or contain mechanisms for recomputation or rehydration from external sources are ideal for ephemeral data use.

Common scenarios include transient data processing pipelines, ephemeral job execution environments, or temporary buffers for microservices.

Contrasting ephemeral data, persistent volumes represent stable storage resources designed to outlive individual pods, providing durability and consistency for application data. Persistent volumes (PVs) in K3s are abstractions over physical storage backends and are crucial when state continuity is vital, as with databases, user-generated content, or long-running services.

Persistent storage in K3s is provisioned via PersistentVolume-Claims (PVCs), which allow pods to request storage resources abstracted from the underlying infrastructure. These volumes typically utilize one or more of the following storage classes, though K3s's lightweight nature advocates for streamlined storage integrations:

- **Network-attached storage (NAS)**: Such as NFS or SMB, providing shared, reliable access.

- **Block storage**: Via cloud provider volumes or local persistent disks.

- **Embedded storage solutions**: Lightweight filesystems like SQLite behind persistent mounts.

The lifecycle of persistent data is decoupled from pod lifecycle:

- Persistent volumes remain available after pod termination or rescheduling, preventing data loss.

- PVCs can be retained, deleted, or recycled depending on configured reclaim policies.

- This durability supports scalable, highly available applications that require stable state between pod restarts or upgrade cycles.

The ephemeral-persistent data dichotomy imposes specific architecture patterns on K3s clusters:

- **Data Durability**: Ephemeral volumes relinquish all stored data upon pod deletion, rendering cluster states vulnerable to unplanned disruptions unless application-level redundancy or external synchronization is employed. Persistent volumes provide the foundation for stable long-term storage, enabling reliable recovery and scaling.

- **Storage Performance**: Ephemeral storage yields superior I/O performance due to its locality, whereas persistent volumes might incur network latency or overhead. Performance-sensitive workloads that do not require data continuity may benefit from ephemeral strategies.

- **Resource Management**: Persistent storage involves allocation and quota management managed by Kubernetes storage classes, necessitating careful planning to avoid bottlenecks. Ephemeral storage, tied to node capacity and pod lifespan, needs monitoring to prevent resource exhaustion.

- **Resilience to Failure**: When nodes fail, ephemeral data on local disks is lost; however, persistent volumes provisioned over redundant storage remain accessible. Cluster resilience strategies must incorporate storage redundancy when persistent state is essential.

Application architects must identify data persistence requirements early to align workload design with storage capabilities:

- **Stateless microservices** can fully rely on ephemeral volumes for caching and logs, delegating critical data persistence to external databases or storage services. This simplifies scaling and recovery.

- **Stateful applications**, such as databases or message queues, mandate persistent volumes for durability and consistency. Leveraging K3s's support for dynamic provisioning where possible simplifies management.

- **Batch processing jobs** that generate large intermediate datasets without long-term value benefit from ephemeral local storage to maximize throughput without incurring storage costs.

- **Logging and monitoring agents** commonly utilize ephemeral storage for transient buffering before shipping data to persistent backends, balancing local performance and eventual durability.

Establishing clear conventions and automation around volume claiming, backup strategies, and failure recovery ensures that ephemeral and persistent data layers coexist without compromising operational goals.

Understanding and correctly architecting data storage strategies in K3s considering the ephemeral-persistent divide directly influences cluster robustness, operational complexity, and application reliability. Efficient use of ephemeral volumes can reduce overhead and improve performance for noncritical data, while persistent volumes are indispensable for application state integrity and long-term data management. Cluster operators should integrate these distinctions into resource provisioning, monitoring, and disaster recovery workflows to optimize infrastructure utilization and service continuity.

5.2. Configuring Volumes and StorageClasses

K3s, as a lightweight Kubernetes distribution, provides full support for Kubernetes storage primitives, enabling flexible, persistent data storage across diverse environments ranging from single-node setups to clustered edge or cloud deployments. Central to persistent storage management are three core resources: *PersistentVolume* (PV), *PersistentVolumeClaim* (PVC), and *StorageClass*. Their appropriate configuration is crucial for efficient storage consumption from local devices, networked file systems, or cloud volumes.

A **PersistentVolume** abstracts a piece of storage in the cluster, which can be provisioned manually or dynamically. It encapsulates details such as the storage provider, capacity, access modes, and reclaim policy. Users request storage through **PersistentVolumeClaims**, which specify capacity and access requirements without tightly coupling to particular physical storage. Finally, **StorageClasses** define the provisioning parameters, including which provisioner to use, reclaim policy defaults, and volume binding modes, enabling dynamic provisioning of PVs.

Local Storage Configuration

Local storage in K3s leverages attached disks or directories on node file systems, typically suited for single-node or edge environments where simplicity and performance are paramount. Local PVs expose a direct path on the host node, so workloads using these volumes require scheduling constraints to ensure pod placement on the appropriate node.

A sample `PersistentVolume` definition for local storage looks like this:

```
apiVersion: v1
kind: PersistentVolume
metadata:
  name: local-pv
spec:
  capacity:
    storage: 10Gi
  volumeMode: Filesystem
  accessModes:
    - ReadWriteOnce
  persistentVolumeReclaimPolicy: Retain
  storageClassName: local-storage
  local:
```

```
    path: /mnt/disks/vol1
  nodeAffinity:
    required:
      nodeSelectorTerms:
      - matchExpressions:
        - key: kubernetes.io/hostname
          operator: In
          values:
          - k3s-node-01
```

In this example, the volume is backed by a local directory /mnt/disks/vol1 on the node k3s-node-01. The nodeAffinity directive guarantees pods requesting this PV are scheduled only on the node where the volume physically resides.

To enable dynamic provisioning of local volumes, a StorageClass references the local persistent volume provisioner, if installed:

```
apiVersion: storage.k8s.io/v1
kind: StorageClass
metadata:
  name: local-storage
provisioner: rancher.io/local-path
volumeBindingMode: WaitForFirstConsumer
reclaimPolicy: Delete
```

The volumeBindingMode: WaitForFirstConsumer delays volume binding and provisioning until a pod is scheduled, enabling proper node affinity resolution in multi-node clusters. The rancher.io/local-path provisioner is the default in K3s for local path volumes, simplifying usage.

Networked Storage Integration

Networked storage, such as NFS or iSCSI, decouples storage from node lifecycles, providing better availability for multi-node clusters. Using NFS as an example, an existing NFS server exports a shared directory accessible by all nodes.

Here is a PV manifest for an NFS volume:

```
apiVersion: v1
kind: PersistentVolume
metadata:
  name: nfs-pv
```

```
spec:
  capacity:
    storage: 20Gi
  accessModes:
    - ReadWriteMany
  persistentVolumeReclaimPolicy: Retain
  storageClassName: nfs
  nfs:
    server: 10.0.0.20
    path: "/exported/path"
```

This PV supports the ReadWriteMany mode, allowing multiple pods across nodes to read and write concurrently to the shared storage.

Corresponding StorageClass for dynamic provisioning is generally not available for vanilla NFS, but specific provisioners like nfs-subdir-external-provisioner may be deployed to automate provisioning on top of NFS infrastructure.

Pods consume this storage by creating PersistentVolumeClaims that reference the appropriate storage class or PV directly:

```
apiVersion: v1
kind: PersistentVolumeClaim
metadata:
  name: nfs-pvc
spec:
  accessModes:
    - ReadWriteMany
  resources:
    requests:
      storage: 5Gi
  storageClassName: nfs
```

When bound, pods mounting this PVC gain access to the shared network file system transparently.

Cloud-Accessed Storage

K3s runs seamlessly on cloud clusters, leveraging cloud provider block storage or shared file systems. Configuration depends on cloud provider CSI drivers-Container Storage Interface implementations that expose cloud storage APIs to Kubernetes.

For example, in AWS with the EBS CSI driver, a `StorageClass` might be:

```
apiVersion: storage.k8s.io/v1
kind: StorageClass
metadata:
  name: gp2
provisioner: ebs.csi.aws.com
parameters:
  type: gp2
  fsType: ext4
reclaimPolicy: Delete
volumeBindingMode: WaitForFirstConsumer
```

Dynamic provisioning allows automatic creation of EBS volumes when PVCs are requested:

```
apiVersion: v1
kind: PersistentVolumeClaim
metadata:
  name: ebs-pvc
spec:
  accessModes:
    - ReadWriteOnce
  storageClassName: gp2
  resources:
    requests:
      storage: 50Gi
```

In multi-cloud environments or when using different providers, selecting and applying proper CSI drivers is essential. K3s facilitates this by allowing easy deployment of these CSI drivers as Helm charts or manifests. The `volumeBindingMode:` `WaitForFirstConsumer` arrangement ensures volumes are provisioned in the same availability zone as the consuming pod, avoiding cross-zone latency or access issues.

Summary of Consumption Workflow

The typical workflow for consuming storage in K3s involves the following steps:

1. Define a `StorageClass` to represent storage provisioning parameters for a desired provider, local or remote.

2. Request resources via a `PersistentVolumeClaim` referencing the `StorageClass`, specifying capacity and access modes.

3. Kubernetes dynamically provisions and binds a matching `PersistentVolume`.

4. The pod specifying the PVC mounts the volume transparently to persist data.

This modular and declarative approach decouples storage management from pod lifecycles and underlying infrastructure details, enabling flexible, scalable, and portable storage consumption patterns across heterogeneous deployment contexts in K3s.

Advanced Considerations

- **Reclaim Policies** (`Retain`, `Delete`, `Recycle`) govern the behavior of PV cleanup after PVC deletion, critical for managing data lifecycle and avoiding unintended data loss.

- **Access Modes**-`ReadWriteOnce`, `ReadOnlyMany`, and `ReadWriteMany`-control the concurrency and pod access semantics to volumes and affect availability models.

- **Volume Binding Mode**-`Immediate` or `WaitForFirstConsumer`-dictates when volume allocation and binding happens, impacting scheduling and zoning constraints.

K3s supports all these Kubernetes primitives with the simplicity and small footprint expected at the edge or lightweight cloud, while retaining extensibility and flexibility characteristic of standard Kubernetes persistent storage. Proper storage configuration enables robust stateful application deployments adapted to various operational scenarios.

5.3. Container Storage Interface (CSI) in K3s

The Container Storage Interface (CSI) is a crucial abstraction layer designed to enable consistent and extensible storage provisioning across diverse container orchestration platforms. K3s, a lightweight Kubernetes distribution tailored for edge and resource-constrained environments, integrates CSI to leverage various external and cloud-native storage solutions without compromising its minimal footprint. This integration ensures that persistent storage in K3s clusters remains flexible, scalable, and interoperable.

K3s incorporates CSI by embedding a configurable CSI provisioner and driver framework into its deployment. Unlike standard Kubernetes distributions where CSI plugins often require explicit installation and complex configuration, K3s streamlines this process by including a default CSI provisioner, `csi-provisioner`, and a set of select drivers within its helm-chart-managed components. This facilitates an opinionated yet extensible storage stack that users can adapt depending on their environment and storage backend.

CSI Driver Selection and Setup

K3s supports various CSI drivers, ranging from cloud-provider specific solutions (e.g., AWS EBS, Azure Disk) to popular open-source drivers (e.g., NFS, Ceph, Longhorn). The selection and activation of a CSI driver in K3s primarily depend on one of two approaches:

- **Built-in drivers**: Some CSI drivers come pre-installed or are automatically deployed with K3s via the server image manifests. These include drivers optimized for local and lightweight scenarios, such as `local-path-provisioner`.

- **External driver deployment**: Users can deploy additional CSI drivers manually or through Helm charts to support specialized storage technologies. This method is necessary for complex backends like Ceph RBD or cloud block storage.

For example, to enable the Local Path Provisioner, which serves as a default CSI driver in K3s for local disk volumes, it can be installed and configured via the embedded Helm chart:

```
kubectl apply -f https://raw.githubusercontent.com/rancher/local-
    path-provisioner/master/deploy/local-path-storage.yaml
kubectl patch storageclass local-path -p '{"metadata": {"
    annotations":{"storageclass.kubernetes.io/is-default-class
    ":"true"}}}'
```

This provisioner uses host paths on nodes to create PersistentVolumes dynamically, offering an efficient storage solution for development and testing environments, as well as small-scale production workloads.

CSI Components in K3s Architecture

K3s embeds essential CSI components, including the CSI Controller, Node Plugin, and Sidecars. These conform to the CSI specification version 1.5+, ensuring compatibility with mainstream Kubernetes workloads. The controller typically runs as a Deployment, managing volume attachments, provisioning requests, and snapshotting operations, whereas the node plugin operates as a DaemonSet, interacting closely with the underlying host to handle volume mounts and unmounts.

A notable architectural consideration is K3s's consolidation of control plane components to reduce resource usage. This has implications for CSI operation, such as limited parallelism in CSI provisioning and potential latency in volume attachment due to fewer controller instances. However, the built-in CSI controller remains functional for typical use cases, with scalability enhanced through clustering and multi-node setups.

Limitations and K3s-Specific Quirks

Although K3s's CSI integration provides substantial benefits, several nuances and constraints arise from its lightweight design philosophy:

- **Storage Class Defaults**: K3s sets `local-path` as the default StorageClass for persistent volumes unless customized. This may not suit all production environments, especially when distributed storage is required.

- **Driver Completeness**: While K3s supports many CSI drivers, some remain incompatible or require manual adaptation due to differences in networking, security policies, or lack of necessary kernel modules in minimal operating systems.

- **Node Limitations**: K3s nodes often run on lower-powered or ARM-based hardware, potentially constraining CSI driver performance, especially for resource-intensive storage backends.

- **Upgrades and Compatibility**: Upgrading CSI drivers within K3s clusters can sometimes require manual reconciliation due to in-place changes in embedded manifests or Helm chart versions, necessitating careful version tracking.

- **Volume Lifecycle Management**: Some CSI features, such as volume snapshotting or cloning, might have partial support depending on the deployed driver and K3s's version.

Example: Enabling Ceph CSI on K3s

Deploying the Ceph RADOS Block Device (RBD) CSI driver on a K3s cluster demonstrates the process of integrating an external, production-grade CSI driver. The steps involve installing the RBD CSI driver components and configuring secret credentials for Ceph authentication:

```
kubectl create namespace ceph-csi

helm repo add ceph-csi https://charts.ceph.com
helm repo update

helm install ceph-csi-rbd ceph-csi/ceph-csi \
  --namespace ceph-csi \
  --set rbd.enabled=true \
```

```
--set rbd.clusterID=<cluster-id> \
--set rbd.cephConfig=config.yaml \
--set rbd.secretNamespace=ceph-csi \
--set rbd.secretName=ceph-secret
```

After this, a StorageClass referencing the deployed Ceph RBD CSI driver is created, specifying parameters such as pool name and image format. PersistentVolumeClaims (PVCs) can then request storage from this backend, and K3s will orchestrate the provisioning per the CSI standard.

```
apiVersion: storage.k8s.io/v1
kind: StorageClass
metadata:
  name: ceph-rbd
provisioner: rbd.csi.ceph.com
parameters:
  pool: rbd
  imageFormat: "2"
  imageFeatures: layering
  csi.storage.k8s.io/provisioner-secret-name: ceph-secret
  csi.storage.k8s.io/provisioner-secret-namespace: ceph-csi
reclaimPolicy: Delete
allowVolumeExpansion: true
volumeBindingMode: Immediate
```

These manifests exemplify the modularity of K3s's CSI support, enabling users to extend storage capabilities without modifying core K3s binaries.

Summary of Best Practices

To maximize CSI usage in K3s, operators should:

- Explicitly define the StorageClass to match application requirements and underlying infrastructure.

- Validate CSI driver compatibility with the host OS and architecture, especially in ARM or minimal Linux distributions.

- Monitor resource consumption of CSI components, tuning replica counts and resource limits accordingly.

- Leverage official Helm charts or manifests from trusted

sources to manage driver lifecycle.

- Test volume attachment, detach, and snapshot operations extensively before deploying into production.

The integration of the Container Storage Interface within K3s reflects the balance between maintaining a minimal Kubernetes footprint and providing versatile, enterprise-grade persistent storage. By supporting CSI, K3s extends its applicability to complex storage environments, facilitating stateful workloads across heterogeneous deployments with confidence and consistency.

5.4. Edge and IoT Storage Patterns

Edge and Internet of Things (IoT) environments introduce unique challenges to storage system design due to their distributed nature and frequent reliance on intermittent or unreliable connectivity. Unlike traditional centralized data centers, edge nodes often operate autonomously with limited resources, necessitating specialized storage patterns that optimize local data management while enabling eventual synchronization with cloud or data center infrastructures. Analyzing storage topologies and appropriate synchronization strategies is critical to ensuring data fidelity, availability, and performance in these constrained settings.

A common topology in edge and IoT storage is the *multi-tiered hierarchical model*, which arranges storage layers geographically and functionally. At the lowest tier are edge devices—ranging from sensors and embedded systems to gateways—storing raw or preprocessed data locally. The middle tier consists of edge servers or micro data centers that aggregate and coordinate data from multiple edge nodes. Finally, the top tier includes centralized cloud or enterprise data repositories responsible for long-term storage, complex analytics, and global data integration.

This tiered structure requires robust mechanisms for data synchronization to handle intermittent connectivity between tiers. *Optimistic replication* techniques are commonly employed, where local writes proceed independently with conflict resolution deferred until synchronization. Conflict-free Replicated Data Types (CRDTs) exemplify data structures designed for such environments, enabling convergent merges without requiring coordination during writes. Their commutative and associative properties facilitate eventual consistency guarantees despite network partitions.

Caching is another central component in edge and IoT storage. Due to bandwidth and latency constraints, edge nodes maintain local caches of both sensor data and configuration metadata. These caches must efficiently manage staleness and consistency, often using time-to-live (TTL) policies or version vector metadata to detect and resolve discrepancies. Write-back caching, wherein updates are initially logged locally and flushed in batches when connectivity is available, balances responsiveness and bandwidth utilization.

Data aggregation at the edge minimizes the volume of data transferred upstream. Aggregation patterns include *in-network processing*, where edge nodes perform computations such as filtering, summarization, or anomaly detection on sensor streams before forwarding results. This reduces storage demands and communication overhead, enabling more scalable and responsive systems. Aggregation also provides opportunities for temporal and spatial data compression, with techniques such as delta encoding or sketches preserving essential features while minimizing footprint.

To illustrate synchronization in intermittently connected environments, consider a distributed edge storage scenario where multiple gateways collect environmental sensor data regionally. Each gateway maintains a local store and periodically synchronizes with a cloud repository. The synchronization process typically employs a *log-based replication* protocol, where updates are appended locally with metadata timestamps or vector clocks. Upon reconnection, the gateways exchange update logs, and a reconciliation algorithm detects conflicts, merges state, and propagates confirmed changes downstream.

```python
class EdgeStore:
    def __init__(self):
        self.local_log = []
        self.state = {}

    def local_write(self, key, value, timestamp):
        self.local_log.append((key, value, timestamp))
        self.state[key] = (value, timestamp)

    def synchronize(self, remote_log):
        combined_log = merge_logs(self.local_log, remote_log)
        self.state = resolve_conflicts(combined_log)
        self.local_log = combined_log

def merge_logs(local, remote):
    # Merge update logs based on timestamps or vector clocks
    return sorted(local + remote, key=lambda x: x[2])

def resolve_conflicts(log):
    resolved_state = {}
    for key, value, timestamp in log:
        if key not in resolved_state or timestamp >
    resolved_state[key][1]:
            resolved_state[key] = (value, timestamp)
    return resolved_state
```

Such synchronization must be resilient to partial update transfers and duplicates, often requiring idempotent or commutative update operations. Metadata overhead for tracking versions and update causality presents a trade-off with resource-constrained devices. Lightweight solutions prioritize minimal metadata, typically relying on scalar timestamps or hybrid logical clocks when vector clocks are infeasible.

Edge and IoT storage patterns also address fault tolerance through *local persistence* combined with delayed consistency. Persistent queues and durable logs ensure data durability during network outages and power failures. Storage components are often optimized for flash memory or other non-volatile storage mediums, emphasizing wear leveling and power efficiency.

The *publish-subscribe* paradigm is frequently employed to decouple data producers and consumers in edge networks. Edge devices publish data updates to local brokers, which cache messages until consumers reconnect. Topic-based subscription models, together with retained messages, enable asynchronous data distribution resilient to intermittent connections.

Lastly, privacy and security in edge storage significantly influence pattern selection. Data minimization at the edge—aggregating and anonymizing sensor data before transmission—is increasingly combined with *secure enclaves* or trusted execution environments to protect sensitive information locally. Encryption for both stored data and synchronization messages is essential, with key management adapted to the decentralized and occasionally disconnected nature of edge deployments.

Storage patterns suitable for edge and IoT environments exhibit a strong emphasis on local autonomy, eventual consistency, and bandwidth-efficient synchronization. Optimistic replication, caching strategies, and data aggregation collectively enable practical and scalable data management despite intermittent connectivity. These approaches form the foundation of resilient, adaptive distributed storage architectures tailored for the dynamic demands characteristic of edge computing.

5.5. Backup, Restore, and Disaster Recovery

Ensuring the resilience of a K3s cluster demands a comprehensive approach to backup, restore, and disaster recovery processes, safeguarding both cluster state and persistent volumes. Given the lightweight nature of K3s and its typical deployment in edge or resource-constrained environments, selecting appropriate tools and designing resilient strategies is critical for business continuity.

Backup Tools and Strategies for K3s

The core cluster state in K3s is managed by etcd (or an alternative datastore) which houses all cluster configurations, secrets, and metadata. Approximately two main categories of backup tools exist:

- **etcdctl snapshots**: The etcdctl command-line utility provides native snapshot functionality to capture the entire etcd datastore state at a point in time.

- **Third-party backup controllers**: Solutions such as Velero extend backup capabilities, providing snapshots for cluster resources and persistent volumes, including advanced features like incremental backups and cloud storage integration.

For etcdctl-based backups, running the following command on the server node creates a snapshot file:

```
etcdctl snapshot save /path/to/backup.db \
  --endpoints=https://127.0.0.1:2379 \
  --cacert=/var/lib/rancher/k3s/server/tls/etcd/server-ca.crt \
  --cert=/var/lib/rancher/k3s/server/tls/etcd/server.crt \
  --key=/var/lib/rancher/k3s/server/tls/etcd/server.key
```

The snapshot file captures the consistent key-value state of the etcd datastore and forms the foundation for total cluster state recovery.

Snapshotting Persistent Volumes

While the etcd snapshot preserves cluster metadata, persistent volume (PV) data requires separate snapshot mechanisms, as applications often maintain critical state in their storage backends. Two strategies dominate:

- **Storage provider snapshot features:** Most modern Container Storage Interface (CSI) drivers support volume snapshots; these leverage underlying block storage capabilities, such as AWS EBS, Azure Disks, or local

LVM snapshots. This approach benefits from hardware-accelerated, application-consistent snapshots if coordinated correctly.

- **Application-level backup**: For stateful applications (e.g., databases), performing logical backups (e.g., mysqldump, pg_dump) ensures fine-grained recovery, especially useful when snapshot mechanisms are unavailable or inconsistent.

Implementing volume snapshot classes and snapshot content manifests enables seamless integration with the K3s PV lifecycle.

Consistent Backup Workflows

A key challenge lies in coordinating etcd and volume snapshots to maintain cluster consistency. Consider the following workflow techniques:

- **Quiesce cluster state**: Temporarily pause disruptive workloads or scale down stateful applications to a steady state to avoid inconsistent writes during snapshot creation.

- **Capture etcd snapshot**: Execute a snapshot of the control-plane datastore while the cluster is quiesced.

- **Create PV snapshots**: Trigger CSI snapshots across relevant persistent volumes, ensuring atomicity if supported by the underlying storage backend.

- **Resume workloads**: Restore normal application operations after confirming snapshot completion.

Automating these steps via Kubernetes Operators or custom controllers reduces human error and improves recovery fidelity.

Node-Local versus Remote Backup and Recovery

Given K3s's frequent deployment at edge locations, backup storage location critically affects recovery strategies:

- **Node-Local Backup**: In environments lacking reliable network connectivity, storing backups locally on the master node or dedicated backup storage attached to the node is common. Benefits include reduced backup latency, network independence, and simpler snapshot orchestration. However, node-local storage risks permanent data loss if node hardware fails or is compromised. To mitigate this, periodic offloading to remote repositories during windows of network availability remains best practice.

- **Remote Backup and Offsite Replication**: For robust disaster recovery, especially to protect against site-wide failures, backups should be replicated to remote, secure storage such as:

  - Cloud object stores (e.g., Amazon S3, Azure Blob Storage)
  - Remote NFS or distributed filesystems
  - Dedicated backup infrastructures with redundancy

  Tools like Velero can natively interface with cloud storage services, enabling encrypted, scheduled uploads of both cluster resource manifests and volume snapshots.

Restore Procedures and Business Continuity

Restoration begins with reestablishing cluster state from the `etcd` snapshot. This involves either:

- Restoring `etcd` from snapshot on a clean K3s installation: This resets the cluster metadata to the exact prior state.

- Incrementally recreating cluster state via manifest apply processes for selective resource restore.

Restoring persistent volumes requires either:

- Reinstating the volume snapshot to the backend storage, followed by volume reattachment.

- Redeploying application-level restores using logical backups.

Command-line example for restoring `etcd` from snapshot:

```
etcdctl snapshot restore /path/to/backup.db \
  --name restored-etcd \
  --data-dir /var/lib/rancher/k3s/server/db/etcd-new \
  --initial-cluster restored-etcd=https://localhost:2380 \
  --initial-cluster-token etcd-cluster-1 \
  --initial-advertise-peer-urls https://localhost:2380
```

Subsequently, the K3s server is configured to use the restored data directory.

Best Practices for Reliable Disaster Recovery

- **Regular and automated backups**: Establish frequent backup schedules aligned with recovery point objectives (RPOs).

- **Test restore procedures**: Periodically validate backup integrity and perform restoration drills to uncover procedural gaps.

- **Encryption and access control**: Secure backups via encryption both at rest and in transit; restrict access to backup artifacts to minimize insider threats.

- **Separation of backup storage**: Maintain backup repositories on isolated infrastructure to reduce risks of common-mode failures.

- **Versioning and retention policies**: Retain multiple backup versions to enable rollback in case of data corruption or ransomware incidents.

- **Document recovery steps**: Maintain comprehensive, up-to-date documentation detailing recovery workflows under various failure scenarios.

These measures collectively underpin operational resilience, ensuring that K3s clusters can withstand and rapidly recover from hardware failures, software errors, or catastrophic events without significant disruption to business services.

5.6. Encryption and Secrets Management

Securing sensitive data within storage backends remains a pivotal aspect of maintaining confidentiality, integrity, and compliance in Kubernetes environments such as K3s. This section delineates the core mechanisms employed to protect secrets at rest, including native encryption techniques, sealing approaches, and the integration of external key management systems (KMS). It further articulates compliance challenges and best practices for minimizing risk in secret handling within K3s clusters.

Encryption at Rest Mechanisms

At-rest encryption involves encoding stored data to ensure its confidentiality against unauthorized access. In Kubernetes, secrets and other sensitive objects stored in etcd or alternative storage backends must be encrypted to mitigate risks such as data exfiltration or insider threats. K3s leverages Kubernetes' built-in support for *encryption providers* configured through the EncryptionConfiguration resource.

A typical at-rest encryption configuration for K3s specifies encryption providers in a hierarchy to sequentially encrypt resource types like Secrets, ConfigMaps, and ServiceAccount tokens. The most secure provider, aescbc or aesgcm, uses strong AES algorithms with 256-bit keys, applied in CBC or GCM modes. The configuration is expressed in YAML and mounted on the K3s API server to enable transparent encryption and decryption.

```
apiVersion: apiserver.config.k8s.io/v1
kind: EncryptionConfiguration
resources:
  - resources:
```

```
    - secrets
  providers:
    - aescbc:
        keys:
          - name: key1
            secret: base64encoded256bitkey==
    - identity: {}
```

The identity provider acts as a fallback to leave data unencrypted if required by compatibility. Keys must be rotated periodically and managed in a secure environment. Failure to enable encryption at rest leaves secrets in etcd as plaintext, which is a critical vulnerability in multi-tenant or untrusted infrastructure scenarios.

Sealing of Secrets and the Role of Sealed Secrets

Directly storing plaintext secrets, even when encrypted within the cluster, can lead to operational risk during transit or backup states. Sealed Secrets offer a complementary approach by encrypting secrets specifically for a single cluster, enabling safe storage in version-controlled repositories without exposing sensitive data.

The sealing process utilizes a public key cryptographic system where the cluster controller holds the private key to decrypt and reconstruct the original secret. The developer encrypts the secret manifest using the cluster's public key via a command-line tool:

```
kubeseal --controller-name=k3s-sealed-secrets-controller \
  --controller-namespace=kube-system < secret.yaml > sealedsecret
    .yaml
```

This sealed secret can then be safely committed to Git. Upon applying the sealed secret manifest to the cluster, the controller decrypts it and creates a standard Kubernetes Secret resource. This methodology enforces *secret immutability and scoped decryption*, preventing accidental leakage and easing compliance with secure software supply chain practices.

Integration with External Key Management Systems

While K3s ships with built-in encryption providers, key management is often a critical element requiring integration with dedicated External Key Management Systems (KMS) for compliance and operational scaling. External KMS services such as AWS KMS, HashiCorp Vault, Google Cloud KMS, or Azure Key Vault provide hardware security module (HSM)-backed key storage, centralized auditability, and fine-grained access policies.

K3s can be configured to utilize an external KMS provider via the Kubernetes KMSEncryptionProvider interface. This setup allows the control plane to delegate encryption key operations, including generation, rotation, and decryption, to the external service. This significantly lowers the risk footprint because the K3s server never persistently stores key material beyond a secure session.

A simplified example of configuring a KMS provider with the Kubernetes API server looks like:

```
apiVersion: apiserver.config.k8s.io/v1
kind: EncryptionConfiguration
resources:
  - resources:
      - secrets
    providers:
      - kms:
          name: aws-kms
          endpoint: unix:///tmp/kms-plugin.sock
      - identity: {}
```

The KMS plugin runs as a gRPC endpoint, mediating all key requests. This model satisfies high compliance regimes demanding key lifecycle control, separation of duties, and non-repudiation.

Compliance Considerations

Data sovereignty, regulatory frameworks such as HIPAA, PCI DSS, and GDPR, and organizational security policies impose stringent requirements on secret management. Encryption at rest shields data from physical theft or unauthorized file access, but encryption configurations must align with compliance mandates specifying encryption algorithms, key length, rotation frequency, and access controls.

Auditing and logging access to secret data further support compliance, although Kubernetes native auditing requires extensions or integrations for comprehensive traceability. K3s clusters operating in regulated environments are encouraged to integrate with enterprise-grade audit and policy enforcement frameworks to fulfill compliance requirements effectively.

Storing secrets outside the cluster in sealed or external secret stores promotes stronger governance and minimizes risk by reducing the attack surface. Furthermore, the effective isolation of key material using external KMS solutions addresses the principle of least privilege, ensuring that secret data remains confidential even in the event of cluster compromises.

Risk Minimization Best Practices

Minimizing risk when managing secrets in K3s involves multiple defense-in-depth strategies:

- Enable encryption at rest by default and verify encryption configurations regularly.

- Leverage sealed secrets or external secret management tools to avoid embedding plaintext secrets in source control.

- Implement external KMS integration for hardware-backed key storage and robust key lifecycle management.

- Enforce strict role-based access controls (RBAC) to limit who can access or modify secrets.

- Automate key rotation to minimize exposure in the event of key compromise.

- Monitor audit logs and set up alerts on suspicious access patterns.

- Reduce secret scope and lifespan by using ephemeral secrets where possible.

Collectively, these practices reduce the attack surface and improve resilience against both external attackers and insider threats. Given that K3s is often deployed in edge or lightweight infrastructures, lightweight but effective encryption and secret management strategies are essential to balance security and operational simplicity.

Encryption and secrets management in K3s involve a layered approach combining built-in encryption at rest, sealed secrets for safe external storage, and integration with external KMS for enterprise-grade security. Considering compliance requirements and applying risk mitigation best practices ensures robust protection of sensitive data across cluster lifecycles.

Chapter 6

Security, Policy, and Compliance in K3s

Security shouldn't be an afterthought—especially in the stream-lined world of K3s. This chapter confronts the unique risks, controls, and policy imperatives that accompany lightweight clusters, equipping you with the practical techniques and tools to defend, govern, and prove compliance no matter where your workloads run.

6.1. Cluster Hardening and Node Security

Cluster hardening in a K3s environment demands meticulous attention to both the operating system and the container orchestration layers to drastically minimize the attack surface while preserving efficiency integral to lightweight Kubernetes distributions. The following principles provide a comprehensive framework to enhance cluster resilience, beginning with OS-level protections, advancing through secure computation baselines, and culminating in actionable security checklists tailored explicitly for K3s nodes.

Operating System-Level Protections

Since K3s is often deployed on resource-constrained or edge nodes, securing the underlying operating system (OS) is paramount. The OS presents the primary attack surface, and a hardened baseline ensures robust defense against breaches:

- **Minimalist OS Installation:** Deploy a minimal and well-maintained operating system, such as Ubuntu Minimal, Alpine, or a secure variant like Container-Optimized OS or Fedora CoreOS. A minimal OS reduces unnecessary services and binaries that could harbor vulnerabilities.

- **Kernel Hardening:** Enable kernel security features such as SELinux or AppArmor for mandatory access control (MAC), seccomp profiles to restrict system calls, and grsecurity patches if available. Disable unneeded kernel modules and enable sysctl parameters to harden network and process isolation:

```
sudo sysctl -w net.ipv4.conf.all.rp_filter=1
sudo sysctl -w kernel.randomize_va_space=2
sudo sysctl -w net.ipv4.tcp_syncookies=1
```

- **Secure Boot and TPM Integration:** Where hardware permits, enable Secure Boot to verify OS integrity at startup, and use TPM modules to store cryptographic keys, reducing tampering risk.

- **Patch Management:** Continuously apply OS and kernel patches through automated tooling or configuration management, ensuring the node remains protected against known vulnerabilities.

- **User and Permission Hardening:** Lock down access by enforcing strict sudo privileges, disabling root logins over SSH, and employing key-based authentication. Regularly audit user accounts and group memberships to eliminate unnecessary access.

Secure Computation Baselines for K3s Nodes

K3s's lightweight design entails specific considerations for safe container runtimes and orchestration components to maintain secure computational environments:

- **Container Runtime Constraints:** Use container runtimes supporting robust isolation mechanisms such as containerd or crio with properly configured seccomp and AppArmor profiles. Limit runtime privileges by default, disallowing root containers and preventing privileged escalation inside pods.

- **Node-Level Pod Security Policies (PSPs) or OPA/-Gatekeeper:** Implement strict Pod Security Admission configurations or utilize Open Policy Agent (OPA) Gatekeeper policies to enforce least privilege pod configurations, disallowing `hostNetwork`, `hostPath` mounts, and privilege escalation unless explicitly required.

- **Secure K3s Service Configuration:** Run the K3s server and agent processes under dedicated system users with minimal privileges, avoid running them as root when feasible, and ensure communication occurs over mutual TLS-encrypted channels using embedded or external certificate management tools.

- **Configuration Drift Prevention:** Employ immutable infrastructure practices by leveraging declarative state management for nodes and pods, minimizing manual configurations which can introduce security holes.

Reducing Attack Surfaces in Minimal Environments

The compact nature of K3s nodes offers both advantage and challenge: fewer components simplify management, but careless additions risk expanding attack vectors. To strategically reduce attack surface:

- **Disable Unused Services and Ports:** Identify and deactivate services unrelated to cluster operation such as legacy network discovery protocols, unused package management daemons, or system utilities that accept inbound network connections.

- **Network Policy Implementation:** Use Kubernetes Network Policies rigorously to restrict intra-cluster traffic only to required namespaces and services, alongside firewall rules on host nodes to limit ingress and egress to trusted sources.

- **Audit and Logging Hardening:** Enable detailed audit logging on both OS and K3s levels, forwarding logs to centralized, tamper-resistant systems. Employ tools like Falco or Sysdig for real-time intrusion detection and abnormal behavior monitoring.

- **Immutable Node Filesystem:** Where possible, configure nodes with read-only root filesystems and overlay filesystems for writable layers, thereby preventing unauthorized persistent changes and simplifying rollback after compromise.

- **Secret Management Hygiene:** Avoid storing sensitive credentials or tokens on the host filesystem. Leverage Kubernetes Secrets with additional encryption at rest, and implement automated key rotation.

- **Automated Security Benchmarking and Compliance:** Integrate CIS Kubernetes Benchmarks and node-specific hardening checks into CI/CD pipelines or regular maintenance cycles to ensure compliance with evolving best practices.

Practical Node Security Checklist for K3s Deployments

The following checklist synthesizes the actionable steps critical for securing K3s nodes while recognizing the constraints of minimal environments:

- **Operating System**

- Deploy minimal, security-focused OS images.
- Configure kernel hardening (SELinux/AppArmor, seccomp).
- Enable Secure Boot and TPM where supported.
- Implement automatic, verified patch management.
- Harden SSH access (disable password, allow keys only).

- **K3s Service and Runtime**

- Run K3s components as non-root users with least privilege.
- Use container runtimes with enforced seccomp and AppArmor policies.
- Enforce strict Pod Security Admission policies or OPA Gatekeeper.
- Enable mutual TLS for all K3s service traffic.

- **Node-Level Network and Process Controls**

- Disable unneeded network ports and services on the node.
- Apply firewall policies restricting node ingress and egress.
- Implement Kubernetes Network Policies for pod isolation.
- Use read-only root filesystems or immutable infrastructure.

- **Monitoring and Incident Response**

- Continuously collect and centralize audit logs.

- Deploy intrusion detection tools like Falco.

- Establish processes for rapid node isolation and recovery.

- **Secrets and Credential Management**

- Store secrets encrypted within Kubernetes Secrets or external vaults.

- Avoid hardcoding credentials on nodes or in containers.

- Rotate cryptographic keys and tokens periodically.

Effective cluster hardening and node security in K3s hinge on a principled reduction of attack vectors without compromising the lightweight ethos. Combining robust OS analogs of traditional security controls with container-native policies and vigilant operational procedures enables a secure, minimal, and highly resilient K3s deployment suitable for diverse production environments.

6.2. RBAC, Admission Controllers, and Pod Security Policies

Role-Based Access Control (RBAC) is the foundational mechanism for enforcing least-privilege access in Kubernetes environments, including lightweight distributions such as K3s. RBAC organizes permissions through the binding of roles to subjects (users, groups, or service accounts), enabling fine-grained control over Kubernetes API resources. Each `Role` or `ClusterRole` enumerates allowed actions expressed as verbs on resource types and API groups. A `RoleBinding` or `ClusterRoleBinding` associates these roles with one or more subjects. This model inherently supports the principle of least privilege by enabling operators to grant only the minimum necessary permissions required for a workload or user to function.

In K3s, the RBAC framework is fully supported and operates compatibly with the upstream Kubernetes API server. However, given K3s' design focus on lightweight operation and simplified management, some default configurations may differ. For instance, K3s bundles a single binary for server components and automates certain roles and bindings for internal components, reducing configuration complexity but also constraining granular customization at boot time. Consequently, administrators should explicitly audit and define RBAC policies to ensure that default bindings do not introduce excessive privileges beyond operational requirements.

Admission controllers serve as dynamic policy enforcement points in the Kubernetes API lifecycle, intercepting resource creation, modification, or deletion requests before persistence. They enable automatic validation, mutation, and policy enforcement on workloads within the cluster. Kubernetes ships with a rich set of built-in admission controllers, but lightweight distributions like K3s include only a subset by default to maintain minimalism and reduce runtime overhead. For example, the `NamespaceLifecycle`, `ResourceQuota`, and `LimitRanger` controllers are typically enabled, while others may require explicit activation if present.

Admission controllers profoundly complement RBAC by enforcing organizational policies contextually, beyond mere permission checks. For instance, dynamic validation ensures that resource specifications comply with security, quota, and operational standards before admission, thus enforcing constraints that RBAC alone cannot express. Implementing custom admission controllers through ValidatingAdmissionWebhook or MutatingAdmissionWebhook allows K3s users to extend control capabilities. However, the webhook approach necessitates additional infrastructure, such as TLS-enabled webservers, which introduces complexity contradictory to the very lightweight design goals of K3s. When deploying admission webhooks on K3s, careful attention must be given to cluster DNS, certificate management, and webhook latency implications.

Pod Security Policies (PSPs) historically provided a cluster-wide mechanism to enforce security constraints on pod specifications, including privilege escalation prevention, volume usage restrictions, and Linux capability controls. PSPs use RBAC to grant or restrict pods based on enforced constraints, effectively acting as admission controllers validating pod spec compliance. However, Kubernetes deprecated PSPs starting in version 1.21 because of inflexibility, complexity, and limited expressive power. In upstream Kubernetes, PSPs have been replaced by the Pod Security Admission controller, which enforces preset security standards ("privileged", "baseline", and "restricted") through namespace labels, offering a simpler management interface.

K3s, as of this writing, does not enable PSPs by default, aligning with broader Kubernetes deprecation trends. Instead, it encourages use of alternative mechanisms such as the Pod Security Admission controller or third-party projects like Open Policy Agent (OPA) Gatekeeper. These alternatives provide more granular, declarative, and extensible security policy enforcement. The Pod Security Admission controller, integrated in K3s by enabling the corresponding admission plugin, leverages namespace annotations to enforce security profiles. This model allows lightweight enforcement without the complexity of custom webhook servers, fitting well within the constraints of K3s' streamlined architecture.

Enforcing least privilege through RBAC combined with admission control mechanisms in K3s demands nuanced consideration of the lightweight platform's constraints. While upstream Kubernetes clusters may enable a broad array of admission controllers and complex PSP configurations, K3s privileges simplicity, which can limit out-of-the-box policy enforcement depth. For critical environments, operators are recommended to selectively enable or deploy admission controllers aligned with their risk posture and automate RBAC role assignments cautiously, ensuring minimal privileges consistent with workload requirements.

Moreover, practitioners should be aware of certain limitations inherent to K3s' design:

- Some admission controllers present in upstream Kubernetes may not be included in K3s or require manual activation, necessitating explicit validation of enabled plugins.

- The bundled single binary approach limits customization of internal controllers, potentially requiring external tooling or sidecar containers for advanced policy enforcement.

- Certificate and webhook management complexity for admission webhook controllers in K3s can outweigh benefits in small clusters, suggesting reliance on built-in mechanisms when feasible.

- The deprecation of PSPs underscores the importance of migrating toward Pod Security Admission or policy engines like OPA Gatekeeper for future-proof security posture in both K3s and upstream Kubernetes.

Effective security enforcement in K3s thus emerges from a deliberate balance between leveraging Kubernetes-native RBAC and admission control features, and adapting to the lightweight platform's operational trade-offs. By utilizing RBAC for strict identity-based permissions combined with admission controllers such as Pod Security Admission or lightweight custom webhooks, cluster operators can achieve nuanced least-privilege enforcement while honoring K3s' design philosophy of reduced resource consumption and simplicity. This layered defense approach mitigates privilege creep and runtime configuration risks, forming a resilient security foundation appropriate for edge, constrained, or development environments where K3s is typically deployed.

6.3. Runtime Protection and Threat Detection

Runtime protection within Kubernetes environments, particularly lightweight distributions like K3s, necessitates efficient tools that operate seamlessly alongside container orchestration mechanisms. Falco and AppArmor represent two pivotal runtime security solutions that provide comprehensive threat detection, mitigation, and monitoring, enabling both reactive and proactive defense strategies in production clusters.

Falco operates as a cloud-native runtime security tool that leverages the Linux kernel's tracing capabilities to monitor system calls made by applications running inside containers. By integrating Falco with a K3s cluster, one can establish a continuous audit mechanism that examines anomalous behavior indicative of runtime threats, such as unexpected file access, abnormal network connections, or unauthorized privilege escalations. Falco's rules engine evaluates these system calls against user-defined or community-curated signatures, generating security events in real time.

The deployment of Falco in a K3s cluster typically involves running it as a DaemonSet, ensuring that every node is continuously monitored. Falco's flexibility allows it to emit alerts through multiple outputs, including standard logs, JSON for SIEM integration, or cloud-based notification channels. This design fosters seamless integration with monitoring and incident response pipelines, essential for early threat detection and mitigation.

AppArmor complements this ecosystem by providing Mandatory Access Control (MAC) on the resource level, restricting the capabilities of running containers through fine-tuned security profiles. Unlike traditional discretionary access control, AppArmor enforces policies that limit process behavior at the kernel level, confining applications to predefined sets of permissions. This confinement limits attack surfaces significantly by preventing exploit activities such as unauthorized file modifications, network communications, or execution of arbitrary binaries.

Within K3s, AppArmor profiles can be applied to pods or individual containers via annotations or admission controllers. This granular approach enables tailored security postures aligned with the principle of least privilege, adapting to the specific operational requirements of workloads. The enforcement modes of AppArmor include complain mode for profiling and learning, and enforce mode for strict access regulation, providing a developmental pathway from policy creation to production hardening.

Audit points form an indispensable component of the security posture facilitated by these runtime tools. These audit points are strategically positioned hooks within the kernel or container runtime to monitor critical security-relevant events. For Falco, audit points consist primarily of system call interceptions captured by eBPF or kernel modules, evidencing activities like file system changes, process creations, and network socket operations. AppArmor utilizes Linux Security Modules hooks to determine whether to allow or deny specific process actions. Together, these audit points generate a granular, high-fidelity view of runtime interactions, essential for comprehensive security monitoring.

The dichotomy of reactive versus proactive protective models manifests distinctly in runtime protection strategies. Reactive models prioritize detection and response, focusing on identifying threats post-facto and triggering mitigation workflows. Falco is predominantly reactive, generating alerts upon the occurrence of suspicious activities, thus enabling security teams to respond promptly to incidents such as intrusion attempts or anomalous process behavior.

Conversely, proactive models emphasize prevention by constraining runtime behavior ahead of time. AppArmor's policy enforcement resides strongly within this paradigm, preventing unauthorized actions by restricting runtime capabilities. By limiting the operational freedom of containers, proactive protection mitigates the risk of exploitation and lateral movement within the cluster. Implementing such policies requires continuous refinement, leveraging audit logs from permissive modes and threat intelligence to evolve profiles without adversely affecting functional requirements.

Effective runtime security within a K3s environment combines these reactive and proactive elements through feedback loops. Audit logs generated by Falco and AppArmor provide critical insights for policy tuning, anomaly baselining, and threat intelligence enrichment. Integrating these tools within Security Information and Event Management (SIEM) systems or orchestration workflows facilitates automated responses, such as blocking suspicious network traffic, quarantining compromised pods, or rolling back untrusted container images.

The resource-efficient nature of K3s necessitates thoughtful consideration when deploying Falco and AppArmor to minimize performance overhead. Configuration parameters, such as filtering rules in Falco or targeted AppArmor profiles, should be optimized to focus on high-risk workloads and critical system calls or capabilities. Moreover, aligning runtime protection tools with Kubernetes-native constructs, such as admission controllers or Pod Security Policies, enhances enforcement consistency across the cluster lifecycle.

The deployment of runtime security tools like Falco and AppArmor in K3s clusters enables layered threat detection and protection by leveraging audit points deeply integrated within the kernel and container runtime. Falco provides real-time, reactive anomaly detection based on comprehensive system call auditing, while AppArmor enforces proactive, kernel-level access control policies that restrict container behavior. Together, these tools establish a robust security framework capable of addressing evolving runtime threats with agility, precision, and minimal operational overhead.

6.4. Secure Supply Chain: Images and Build Pipelines

Ensuring that only trusted container images are deployed in a Kubernetes cluster is a fundamental pillar of a secure supply chain. The introduction of unverified or compromised images risks exposure to vulnerabilities, backdoors, and other attack vectors that can undermine the integrity of the entire platform. Securing this supply chain requires a comprehensive approach that embraces multiple complementary strategies: image provenance verification, vulnerability scanning, cryptographic signing, and rigorous policy enforcement within the cluster environment. Additionally, these security practices must be seamlessly integrated into the DevOps workflows and Continuous Integration/Continuous Deployment (CI/CD) pipelines to maintain agility without sacrificing security.

Image Provenance: Establishing Trust Through Metadata

Image provenance refers to the ability to trace an image back through its creation process, linking it to verified sources, build environments, and configurations. Provenance metadata includes details such as the originating Git commit, build tools and versions, and the base image lineage. This information is crucial for forensic investigations and compliance requirements, and for preventing supply chain attacks that manipulate image contents post-build.

Standard mechanisms such as the Open Container Initiative (OCI) image format support attaching provenance metadata to container images. Emerging specifications like the *in-toto* framework provide structured provenance metadata assertions that describe the artifacts' lifecycle and attest to their integrity. These attestations, stored alongside container images in registries, allow runtime systems to verify that the image was produced via trusted processes and has not been tampered with since creation.

Infrastructure platforms can enforce that only images with verified provenance metadata are allowed to be pulled and deployed in the cluster, effectively blocking images from unknown or untrusted sources.

Vulnerability Scanning: Detecting Flaws Before Deployment

Even trusted sources can sometimes produce images containing security vulnerabilities. Systematic vulnerability scanning of container images is essential to detect known flaws in operating system packages, application dependencies, and runtime configurations.

Modern scanning tools operate by comparing installed packages and binaries in images against extensive vulnerability databases such as the National Vulnerability Database (NVD) or vendor-specific advisories. Common tools include Trivy, Clair, and Anchore Engine, each integrated with container registries or CI/CD pipelines to automate scanning at build time, push time, or pre-deployment.

Scanning results are classified by severity, allowing for policy-based decisions that control whether an image can proceed to deployment. The ability to integrate scanning into the CI/CD pipeline ensures that developers receive immediate feedback and can remediate issues early, minimizing the risk of deploying vulnerable images.

Image Signing: Cryptographic Assurance of Integrity and Origin

Cryptographic signing of container images is a critical practice for assuring the image's integrity and authenticity. Signing uses private keys to generate a signature over the image's content hash, which can later be validated using the corresponding public key before deployment.

Standards such as Docker Content Trust (DCT), based on the Notary v2 protocol, and the more recent *Sigstore* project, have emerged to facilitate industry-wide adoption of signing and verification. Sigstore, in particular, lowers the barrier to entry by automating key management and integrating transparency logs, providing both authenticity and tamper-evident audit trails.

Image signing prevents attacks such as "man-in-the-middle" modification of images during transport and unauthorized image substitution in registries. It enables cluster admission controllers to accept only images signed by approved keys or originating from trusted entities.

Policy Enforcement: Gatekeeping at the Cluster Level

Enforcing image trustworthiness within the Kubernetes cluster is realized through admission controllers and policy engines that verify image signatures, validate provenance metadata, and assess vulnerability scan reports before allowing pod creation.

Tools such as Open Policy Agent (OPA) Gatekeeper, Kyverno, and Kritis enable declarative policy enforcement to centrally define image trust policies. These policies can mandate requirements like:

- Rejection of images lacking valid digital signatures from specified authorities.

- Blocking images exceeding vulnerability severity thresholds.

- Restricting allowed base image registries or namespaces.

- Ensuring that only images with valid provenance attestations can be deployed.

These policy engines integrate with Kubernetes admission webhook mechanisms to provide real-time enforcement, preventing non-compliant images from entering the runtime environment.

Integration with DevOps Workflows and CI/CD Pipelines

Securing the container image supply chain must align with development velocity and continuous delivery paradigms. This calls for embedding security controls within the CI/CD pipelines and development toolchains rather than applying them as isolated or after-the-fact gates.

Typical CI/CD pipeline stages for a secure supply chain include:

1. **Build**: Automated building of images from source code repositories with immutable build environments to ensure reproducibility.

2. **Scan**: Running vulnerability analysis tools and generating detailed reports. Fail builds if critical vulnerabilities are detected.

3. **Sign**: Automatically signing images on successful builds with managed signing keys or Sigstore integration.

4. **Publish**: Pushing images with attached provenance metadata and signatures to a trusted container registry.

5. **Deploy**: Enforced by cluster policies that verify all metadata and signatures before allowing rollout to production.

This integration enables a *shift-left* approach, reducing human error and improving response times to newly discovered vulnerabilities or supply chain threats. Furthermore, telemetry from image scanning and policy enforcement tools provides continuous visibility into the security posture of the deployed applications.

The secure container image supply chain is an ecosystem of layered controls: traceable provenance data supports trust and auditability; continuous vulnerability scanning identifies weaknesses before runtime; cryptographic signing guarantees origin and integrity; and robust policy enforcement at the cluster gate prevents unauthorized images from executing. Embedding these controls into automated CI/CD pipelines aligns security with modern agile development, reducing risks without obstructing innovation or operational speed. Ultimately, this rigor builds resilient infrastructure able to withstand evolving threats in a deeply interconnected software supply landscape.

6.5. Policy Management with OPA and Kyverno

Declarative policy enforcement is a critical mechanism for maintaining security, compliance, and operational governance in Kubernetes environments such as K3s. Open Policy Agent (OPA) and Kyverno represent two prominent frameworks that facilitate policy-as-code, enabling administrators to codify and automate admission control and dynamic compliance reporting. Both integrate with the Kubernetes admission control framework but differ fundamentally in their policy definition approaches and operational paradigms.

Open Policy Agent leverages a high-level declarative language called Rego to express policies. Rego policies are logically structured queries that evaluate Kubernetes resource attributes and environmental variables to yield admission decisions. The OPA server acts as a centralized decision point for policy evaluation, interfacing with Kubernetes Admission Controllers via webhooks. OPA supports complex and context-rich policies, including queries that incorporate temporal constraints, multi-resource relationships, and external data sources.

A typical OPA policy intended for admission control within a K3s cluster might restrict the deployment of Pods exposing privileged containers or enforce namespace-specific resource quota constraints. For instance, consider the following Rego snippet that denies any Pod containing privileged containers:

```
package kubernetes.admission
```

```
deny[msg] {
  input.request.kind.kind == "Pod"
  container := input.request.object.spec.containers[_]
  container.securityContext.privileged == true
  msg := sprintf("privileged container '%s' is not allowed", [
    container.name])
}
```

This policy interrogates the admission request object and generates denial messages when violations occur. Integrating such a policy within K3s involves configuring the Kubernetes Admission Webhook to call the OPA server, thereby achieving real-time enforcement.

Kyverno, in contrast, employs YAML-based declarative policies designed to be native and intuitive to Kubernetes users. It operates as a Kubernetes controller within the cluster and processes policies as Custom Resources. Kyverno facilitates admission control and mutation capabilities directly through familiar Kubernetes manifests without requiring prior knowledge of a dedicated policy language. This ease of use accelerates policy adoption while maintaining robust enforcement features.

A Kyverno policy to enforce similar restrictions on privileged containers could be defined as:

```
apiVersion: kyverno.io/v1
kind: ClusterPolicy
metadata:
  name: disallow-privileged-containers
spec:
  validationFailureAction: enforce
  rules:
  - name: check-privileged
    match:
      resources:
        kinds:
        - Pod
    validate:
      message: "Privileged containers are not allowed."
      pattern:
        spec:
          containers:
          - securityContext:
```

```
privileged: false
```

This policy directly expresses the constraint in Kubernetes resource schema terms, enabling straightforward policy management within the cluster. It simplifies dynamic enforcement and can also perform mutation, such as injecting default labels or annotations, further aiding compliance.

Admission Control Workflow and Policy Application in K3s

K3s, as a lightweight Kubernetes distribution, supports dynamic integration of these policy engines for admission control. Both OPA and Kyverno are deployed as Kubernetes workloads, and their admission webhooks are configured to intercept resource creation and modification requests.

When a user submits a resource manifest to the K3s API server, the following sequence occurs:

- The API server forwards the admission request to configured admission webhooks corresponding to policy engines.

- The policy engine evaluates the request against predefined policies.

- A decision is returned: accept, deny, or mutate.

- Upon acceptance, the resource is persisted; if denied, the user receives a clear rejection message.

- Mutating webhooks modify the request manifest as specified before acceptance.

For example, enforcing network policy compliance may require denying services that expose ports outside an organization's security baseline. Using Rego policies or Kyverno validations, clusters can automatically reject configurations violating such constraints, eliminating manual auditing overhead.

Dynamic Compliance Monitoring and Reporting

Beyond admission-time enforcement, continuous compliance monitoring is essential in regulated environments. Both OPA and Kyverno support real-time compliance reporting mechanisms, although their approaches differ.

OPA can export detailed evaluation metrics and decision logs, enabling centralized analysis via integration with Prometheus, Elasticsearch, or custom dashboards. These logs capture policy evaluation outcomes, resource metadata, and context, facilitating trend detection and audit readiness.

Kyverno supports generating `PolicyReport` Custom Resources that summarize compliance status across namespaces or clusters. PolicyReports are updated dynamically and can be queried using standard Kubernetes tools or integrated with Prometheus exporters, providing operators with up-to-date compliance landscapes. For example, a Kyverno PolicyReport snippet exhibits:

```
apiVersion: wgpolicyk8s.io/v1alpha2
kind: PolicyReport
metadata:
  name: compliance-report
  namespace: default
results:
- policy: disallow-privileged-containers
  resource:
    kind: Pod
    namespace: default
    name: example-pod
  message: "Privileged containers are not allowed."
  status: fail
```

This continuous feedback loop assists DevOps teams and security auditors in maintaining compliance posture without manual intervention.

Comparative Considerations

While both OPA and Kyverno serve similar ends, selection often hinges on organizational priorities and expertise. OPA's modular and expressive Rego policies enable complex, multi-dimensional rules but introduce a steeper learning curve and external dependency management. Kyverno's Kubernetes-native YAML policies provide immediate accessibility and simplified lifecycle management but may have limitations in expressing deeply nested logic or external data integrations.

In K3s environments designed for lightweight operation, Kyverno's in-cluster controller model aligns with minimal external dependencies, while OPA can be optimized to run as a sidecar or external service depending on architectural preferences.

Effective declarative policy enforcement in lightweight Kubernetes environments such as K3s demands a strategic combination of policy specification, admission control integration, and dynamic compliance reporting. OPA and Kyverno exemplify two complementary approaches leveraging policy-as-code for robust security governance. Mastery of their capabilities allows integrating admission-time validation with continuous compliance observability, fostering secure and compliant containerized application delivery pipelines.

6.6. Multi-Tenancy Security Models

In shared Kubernetes environments such as those orchestrated by K3s, implementing robust multi-tenancy security models is critical to maintaining isolation among tenants or workloads. Unlike traditional monolithic clusters, multi-tenant clusters accommodate multiple user groups or applications, each with distinct access rights and security constraints. This section examines secure isolation strategies in K3s clusters, emphasizing namespace design, resource control, and access management, while addressing challenges specific to small, distributed setups.

Tenant isolation in Kubernetes typically relies on logical sepa-
rations via namespaces, complemented by policy enforcement
through Role-Based Access Control (RBAC), network segmentation, and workload-specific constraints. In K3s, a lightweight Kubernetes distribution designed for resource-constrained environments, multi-tenancy must balance security rigor with minimal
overhead.

Three primary isolation models are recognized:

1. **Namespace-based Isolation**: Each tenant operates
   within one or more dedicated namespaces. Kubernetes
   namespaces provide a scoped environment that partitions
   resources such as pods, services, and persistent volumes.
   RBAC policies limit tenant users and applications to act
   solely within their namespaces.

2. **Cluster-based Isolation**: Tenants are assigned distinct
   clusters, which naturally isolates all resources and network
   traffic. However, this model incurs heavier operational
   costs and is generally unsuitable for small distributed setups
   where resource efficiency is paramount.

3. **Hybrid or Virtual Clusters**: This approach leverages
   namespace-based models augmented with admission controllers and network policies to achieve near cluster-level isolation, often using tools such as Virtual Clusters or Project
   Contour.

Given K3s's design goals emphasizing simplicity and low resource
consumption, namespace-based isolation remains the most practical and widely deployed multi-tenancy model.

Namespace design is central to effective multi-tenant security in
K3s. Several best practices emerge from real-world deployments:

One Namespace per Tenant or Workload

Assigning a dedicated namespace per tenant or distinct workload boundary enables straightforward policy application and limits the blast radius of misconfigurations or attacks. Each namespace acts as the fundamental security boundary within the cluster.

Namespace Labeling and Naming Conventions

Consistent labeling schemes and descriptive namespace names aid in automation and policy enforcement. For example, labels such as `tenant=finance` or `environment=production` allow network policies and admission controllers to dynamically group namespaces and apply tenant-specific restrictions.

Resource Quotas and Limits

Defining resource quotas at the namespace level prevents resource starvation and denial-of-service attacks caused by rogue or misbehaving tenants. K3s supports resource quotas for CPU, memory, storage, and object counts, allowing administrators to enforce fair usage across tenants.

Network Policies for Traffic Segmentation

Kubernetes network policies restrict cross-namespace pod communication. For multi-tenancy, these must be carefully crafted to enforce zero-trust principles, permitting traffic flows only when explicitly required. For example, isolating each tenant's namespace network traffic prevents lateral movement within the cluster.

Namespace Scoped Secrets and ConfigMaps

Sensitive information such as credentials, certificates, and configuration data should be tightly scoped to namespaces. RBAC must prevent cross-namespace inspection or modification of these resources.

K3s integrates Kubernetes-standard RBAC to enforce fine-grained access control. For multi-tenancy, the following approaches are recommended:

- **Least Privilege Roles**: Tenant roles should be scoped to namespace resources and verbs necessary for operation. Avoid cluster-wide roles which risk privilege escalation.

- **Group-based Role Assignments**: Aligning Kubernetes RBAC groups with organizational teams enables simplified user management and consistent policy enforcement.

- **Admission Controllers**: Employ admission controllers such as `PodSecurityPolicies` (or their replacements like `Pod Security Admission` in newer Kubernetes versions) to restrict pod capabilities, privilege escalation, and host network access per namespace.

In K3s, custom admission webhooks may be employed sparingly to enforce tenant-specific policies without introducing significant latency or complexity.

Small, distributed K3s clusters-common in edge or IoT deployments-pose unique multi-tenancy challenges:

Limited Compute and Network Resources
Lightweight nodes constrain the overhead possible for policy enforcement agents, network plugins, or sidecars. This limits the complexity and number of network policies and admission controllers feasible without degrading performance.

Minimal Operating Surface for Security Tools
K3s often omits optional components for a minimal footprint, reducing built-in defenses like advanced network plugins capable of enforcing sophisticated policies (e.g., Cilium). Security models must compensate using simpler, native Kubernetes primitives.

Distributed and Intermittent Connectivity
Clusters may span locations with flaky network connections, complicating centralized policy updates and monitoring. Multi-tenant policies must be fail-safe and enable local enforcement when disconnected.

Management and Auditing Constraints

Resource-limited control planes restrict comprehensive logging and auditing. Secure multi-tenancy in these environments necessitates minimal yet sufficient access logging and anomaly detection to identify tenant-related security events.

Isolation Model	Strengths	Limitations in Small K3s
Namespace-Based	Lightweight, native Kubernetes support, scalable	Relies on careful policy design; less robust against namespace escape vulnerabilities
Full Cluster-per-Tenant	Maximum isolation, avoids namespace vulnerabilities	High resource cost; impractical for edge or low-power devices
Virtual Clusters / Project Spaces	Near cluster-level security within shared cluster	Introduces complexity and overhead; may be too heavy for minimal K3s setups

Namespace-based isolation, supplemented with rigorous RBAC, network policies, and resource quotas, represents the optimal balance for multi-tenancy in K3s clusters. It leverages native constructs without imposing undue operational burden.

A canonical setup script snippet for creating a secure namespace with resource quotas and network policy might be expressed as:

```
apiVersion: v1
kind: Namespace
metadata:
  name: tenant-a
  labels:
    tenant: tenant-a
---
apiVersion: v1
kind: ResourceQuota
metadata:
  name: tenant-a-quota
  namespace: tenant-a
spec:
  hard:
    requests.cpu: "2"
    requests.memory: 4Gi
    limits.cpu: "4"
    limits.memory: 8Gi
    pods: "10"
---
apiVersion: networking.k8s.io/v1
```

```
kind: NetworkPolicy
metadata:
  name: default-deny
  namespace: tenant-a
spec:
  podSelector: {}
  policyTypes:
  - Ingress
  - Egress
```

This setup creates a tenant-isolated namespace with capped resource usage and a default deny-all network policy, which forces explicit allowance of communications, enhancing security boundaries.

Designing multi-tenancy security models in K3s demands a careful balance between minimalism and robust isolation. Namespace-centric strategies, fortified with RBAC and network policies, are paramount, particularly in resource-limited, distributed environments. Understanding these nuanced trade-offs enables defenders and operators to maintain strong tenant isolation without compromising K3s's inherent agility and efficiency.

6.7. Audit Logging and Compliance Pipelines

Audit logging in K3s clusters is a critical practice for maintaining security, ensuring operational transparency, and fulfilling regulatory requirements, especially within edge and hybrid cloud environments where distributed deployments introduce distinct challenges. The lightweight design of K3s, while optimized for resource-constrained scenarios, retains compatibility with Kubernetes auditing mechanisms, enabling fine-grained event capture and integration with centralized compliance pipelines.

At the core of audit logging in K3s is the Kubernetes audit framework, which captures detailed records of API server requests, including user identities, timestamps, request metadata, and request outcomes. To enable audit logging, K3s requires configuration of the API server with audit policy files and audit sinks. The audit policy defines the scope and granularity of logged events, allowing administrators to filter by verbs (e.g., create, update, delete), resources (pods, secrets, etc.), or users. For example, a minimal audit policy configuration might be structured as follows:

```
apiVersion: audit.k8s.io/v1
kind: Policy
rules:
  - level: Metadata
    verbs: ["create", "update", "patch", "delete"]
    resources:
      - group: ""
        resources: ["pods", "secrets"]
  - level: None
    users: ["system:kube-proxy"]
```

In K3s, audit logging is enabled by specifying the API server flag `--audit-policy-file` alongside an `--audit-log-path`. Due to the embedded nature of K3s components, these flags are usually configured via the K3s server startup parameters or embedded systemd service files depending on the deployment methodology. The audit logs are typically stored in JSON format to allow structured querying.

Integration with external log aggregation and security information and event management (SIEM) systems is pivotal for scalability and compliance. Common choices include Fluentd, Fluent Bit, Logstash, or OpenTelemetry collectors, which can tail Kubernetes audit logs and forward them to centralized platforms such as Elasticsearch, Splunk, or cloud-based equivalents like AWS Cloud-Watch or Azure Monitor. This externalization facilitates retention policies, real-time alerting, and correlation with broader infrastructure logs, vital for comprehensive incident investigations.

A common pipeline architecture deploys a sidecar or DaemonSet-based log shipper that watches the audit log files and converts them into standard formats such as JSON or the Elastic Common Schema (ECS). This standardization is crucial when supporting multi-cluster, edge, and hybrid architectures where data normalization reduces complexity in downstream analysis.

Designing workflows for regulatory reporting involves establishing traceable chains of custody and automated generation of compliance evidence. Relevant compliance frameworks for edge and hybrid deployments include:

- **PCI DSS (Payment Card Industry Data Security Standard)**: Enforces logging of all access to cardholder data environments, with chain-of-custody mechanisms suitable for edge locations managing point-of-sale devices.

- **HIPAA (Health Insurance Portability and Accountability Act)**: Requires audit trails for Protected Health Information (PHI) access and modifications.

- **GDPR (General Data Protection Regulation)**: Mandates accountability with data access logs and breach investigation capabilities.

- **NIST SP 800-53/800-171**: Defines controls for federal information systems, emphasizing continuous monitoring and audit logs integrity.

K3s audit logs feed compliance workflows by supporting event ingestion into SIEM tools that enforce retention policies aligned with these standards, trigger automated reporting at predefined intervals, and generate alerts on anomalous activities such as unauthorized access or privilege escalations.

In incident investigations, correlating K3s audit logs with system and network telemetry from edge nodes is paramount. These logs provide actors, actions, and outcomes, while network flow data and node metrics give context on lateral movement attempts or resource abuse. To streamline this, emerging compliance pipelines employ machine learning models to flag unusual sequences in audit logs, supported by rich metadata extraction such as user-agent strings, IP addresses, and Kubernetes RBAC bindings.

Handling edge-specific challenges includes dealing with intermittent connectivity to central logging servers, limited local storage, and heightened data privacy requirements. To mitigate data loss, strategies such as local buffering with backpressure-aware forwarders or opportunistic resending during connectivity windows are implemented. Additionally, encryption of audit logs at rest and in transit, combined with strict access controls, ensures confidentiality and integrity.

K3s clusters also benefit from custom audit sinks that enable forwarding logs directly from the API server to remote endpoints, bypassing local filesystems. This can be configured with a webhook-style sink, allowing instant log delivery with minimal latency, essential for real-time compliance monitoring in critical edge environments.

```yaml
apiVersion: auditregistration.k8s.io/v1alpha1
kind: AuditSink
metadata:
  name: remote-webhook
spec:
  policy:
    level: RequestResponse
  webhook:
    throttle:
      qps: 10
      burst: 15
    clientConfig:
      url: https://audit-collector.example.com/webhook
```

Security best practices recommend applying immutability to audit logs, leveraging append-only storage or write-once-read-many (WORM) policies, and cryptographic hashing to detect tampering. Regular reconciliation between audit logs and observed cluster state aids in identifying discrepancies that may signal insider threats or compromised components.

Audit logging in K3s clusters extends traditional Kubernetes security capabilities into resource-constrained edge and hybrid scenarios by combining flexible policy-driven event capture, external log aggregation, and compliance-targeted automation. Establishing robust pipelines that integrate audit data into comprehensive security operations centers ensures adherence to stringent regulatory frameworks while enabling effective incident response and forensic analysis across distributed cloud-native infrastructures.

Chapter 7

Monitoring, Logging, and Observability

How do you truly know what's happening inside your lightweight clusters, especially when they span fleets of devices or distant edges? This chapter peels back the layers of K3s operations, arming you with the clarity, insight, and tooling to anticipate issues, optimize resources, and bring visibility to every corner of your infrastructure.

7.1. Metrics Server and Core Observability Framework

The *Metrics Server* in K3s serves as a fundamental component for resource utilization monitoring across the cluster, enabling observability at both the application and node levels. It is a lightweight, scalable implementation of the Metrics API, designed particularly for resource-constrained environments where K3s is often deployed. The server aggregates critical CPU and memory metrics from the Kubelet running on each node, exposing these data points via the Kubernetes Metrics API. This makes it accessible to standard querying and visualization tools that rely on cluster metrics for operational insight.

The Metrics Server operates by scraping resource usage statistics at regular intervals from the Kubelet Summary API. The collected metrics primarily include CPU cores usage and working set memory, which are essential for managing pod scheduling, autoscaling, and capacity planning. Unlike Prometheus or other scraping agents, the Metrics Server does not persist historical data; instead, it offers near real-time metrics enabling immediate decisions and short-term analysis.

To deploy the Metrics Server in K3s, it is often integrated by default; however, one can verify or customize its operation via the `metrics-server` addon or direct manifest application. Configuration options allow tuning scraping intervals, secure communication, and authorization settings.

Collecting resource data through the Metrics API is straightforward using the Kubernetes CLI tool `kubectl`. For example, fetching live metrics for all pods in the default namespace can be done via:

```
kubectl top pods
```

Similarly, to query node-level metrics:

```
kubectl top nodes
```

These commands internally communicate with the Metrics Server, providing CPU and memory consumption summaries critical for operational diagnostics.

Beyond basic CLI interactions, advanced observability often requires querying and visualizing metrics across time and dimensions. While Metrics Server supplies instantaneous data, it serves as a data source foundation upon which more comprehensive monitoring stacks are built. For example, Prometheus, a time-series database and monitoring tool widely used in Kubernetes ecosystems, can scrape and store cluster metrics over time, enabling historical analysis, alerting, and complex queries.

To enhance observability in K3s, Prometheus can be configured to scrape the Metrics Server or directly interface with Kubelet endpoints. This integrated approach combines the real-time lightweight nature of Metrics Server with the robust data retention and querying capabilities of Prometheus.

Additionally, metrics can be exposed alongside application-specific telemetry using the *Core Observability Framework*, which typically comprises the following components:

- **Metrics Collection**: Metrics Server and Prometheus collaboratively collect cluster and application-level metrics.

- **Log Aggregation**: Tools such as Fluentd or Loki gather and centralize logs for trace correlation and event diagnostics.

- **Tracing**: Distributed tracing systems like Jaeger help analyze application request flows across microservices.

- **Visualization**: Grafana, a visualization platform, consumes Prometheus metrics to create dashboards, offering contextual insights through graphical representations.

The integration of these components forms a cohesive stack, essential for monitoring modern Kubernetes clusters, where understanding performance bottlenecks, scaling behaviors, and anomaly detection demands comprehensive observability.

Practical visualization often involves creating dashboards that track critical resource usage patterns, for instance:

- CPU and memory utilization trends per node or namespace.

- Pod restart and eviction rates signaling stability issues.

- Network throughput and disk I/O metrics informing infrastructure health.

These visualizations empower operators to rapidly pinpoint underperforming components and optimize resource allocation.

To query metrics programmatically, the Prometheus Query Language (PromQL) offers powerful expressions. For example, to calculate the average CPU usage over the last 5 minutes across all pods in a namespace named `production`:

```
avg(rate(container_cpu_usage_seconds_total{namespace="production
   "}[5m]))
```

Such queries can be embedded into alerting rules that trigger notifications when thresholds are breached, ensuring proactive cluster management.

The incorporation of the Metrics Server in K3s supplies an essential observability foundation, furnishing live resource metrics vital for runtime administration and auto-scaling. When combined with complementary telemetry tools-particularly Prometheus for long-term storage, Grafana for visualization, and log/tracing systems for holistic insights-a robust core observability framework emerges. This framework supports both operational efficiency and reliability in containerized environments, adapting to the dynamic resource demands and failure modes inherent in distributed Kubernetes clusters.

7.2. Integrating Prometheus and Grafana

The integration of Prometheus and Grafana establishes a robust monitoring stack tailored for Kubernetes lightweight distributions such as K3s, enabling efficient metrics collection, visualization, and alerting essential for observability at scale. This section elaborates on configuring Prometheus to scrape custom metrics, setting alerting rules, and leveraging Grafana's visualization capabilities, all optimized for the resource constraints and architectural nuances of K3s environments.

Prometheus operates via a pull model, scraping metrics endpoints periodically. In K3s clusters, service discovery differs subtly due to the streamlined control plane and embedded components. To accommodate this, Prometheus should be deployed with a configuration directing it to scrape metrics from core Kubernetes components, critical system pods, and any custom-instrumented applications.

A typical Prometheus `prometheus.yml` configuration adapted to K3s includes Kubernetes service discovery with annotations for automatic scraping:

```
scrape_configs:
  - job_name: 'kubernetes-pods'
    kubernetes_sd_configs:
      - role: pod
        api_servers:
          - 'https://kubernetes.default.svc'
    relabel_configs:
      - source_labels: [
__meta_kubernetes_pod_annotation_prometheus_io_scrape]
        action: keep
        regex: true
      - source_labels: [
__meta_kubernetes_pod_annotation_prometheus_io_path]
        action: replace
        target_label: __metrics_path__
        regex: (.+)
      - source_labels: [__address__,
__meta_kubernetes_pod_annotation_prometheus_io_port]
        action: replace
        regex: ([^:]+)(?::\d+)?;(\d+)
        replacement: $1:$2
        target_label: __address__
```

This configuration directs Prometheus to scrape pods annotated with `prometheus.io/scrape=true`, using the annotated port and path. In K3s, ensure the Prometheus server has access to the Kubernetes API and proper RBAC permissions.

Instrumenting applications with custom metrics enables exposing domain-specific telemetry beyond default Kubernetes and system metrics. Prometheus client libraries are available for popular languages such as Go, Python, Java, and Node.js. Implementing instrumentation follows three primary metric types:

- **Counters**: Monotonic increasing values, e.g., total HTTP requests.

- **Gauges**: Values that can go up and down, e.g., current memory usage.

- **Histograms and Summaries**: Distributions of values, e.g., request durations or payload sizes.

An example in Go to expose HTTP request duration histogram:

```
var (
    httpDuration = prometheus.NewHistogramVec(prometheus.
    HistogramOpts{
        Name: "http_request_duration_seconds",
        Help: "Histogram of HTTP request durations in seconds.",
        Buckets: prometheus.DefBuckets,
    }, []string{"route"})
)

func init() {
    prometheus.MustRegister(httpDuration)
}

func handler(w http.ResponseWriter, r *http.Request) {
    timer := prometheus.NewTimer(httpDuration.WithLabelValues("/
    foo"))
    defer timer.ObserveDuration()
    // Handle request logic
}
```

Deploy the instrumented application as a pod in K3s and annotate its manifest with the scrape annotations for Prometheus discovery. Custom metrics should follow consistent and meaningful naming conventions to facilitate clearer visualization and alerting.

Alerting on critical conditions enables proactive incident response. Prometheus supports alerting via rules defined in YAML files, which evaluate metric expressions continually. For example, to alert when node CPU usage exceeds 85% for five minutes:

```
groups:
- name: node-alerts
  rules:
  - alert: HighCPUUsage
    expr: 100 - (avg by(instance)(rate(node_cpu_seconds_total{
    mode="idle"}[5m])) * 100) > 85
    for: 5m
    labels:
      severity: critical
    annotations:
      summary: "Instance {{ $labels.instance }} CPU usage is
      above 85%"
      description: "CPU usage is sustained over 85% for more than
      5 minutes."
```

Integrating an Alertmanager component allows routing alerts to various receivers such as email, Slack, or PagerDuty. In K3s, this component can be deployed alongside Prometheus or externally, with appropriate alert configurations.

Grafana complements Prometheus by providing a flexible, query-driven dashboard platform. Upon deploying Grafana in K3s, the Prometheus data source can be added via the UI or configuration files, typically pointing to the internal Prometheus service URL like `http://prometheus-server.kube-system.svc.cluster.local:9090`.

Key practices for dashboard creation include:

- **Using PromQL queries**: Construct precise PromQL expressions to extract meaningful trends and aggregate data efficiently.

- **Templating and Variables**: Define templated variables for dynamic filtering (e.g., by namespace, deployment, or pod), enabling reusable and interactive dashboards.

- **Panel Types**: Utilize visual elements such as time series graphs, heatmaps, and single stat panels catering to the metric semantics.

Example PromQL for tracking custom HTTP request duration percentiles:

```
histogram_quantile(0.95, sum(rate(http_request_duration_seconds_bucket[5m]))
by (le))
```

Grafana supports alerting based on dashboard panel thresholds, complementing Prometheus alerts and allowing richer context in notification messages.

Resource Efficiency: Both Prometheus and Grafana must be tuned for low resource consumption suitable for K3s's lightweight design. This includes setting appropriate scraping intervals, retention policies, and enabling storage compaction on Prometheus.

Security Considerations: Secure communication between Prometheus, Alertmanager, Grafana, and Kubernetes API server should use TLS with proper certificates. RBAC permissions must be minimal but sufficient for Prometheus service accounts to query cluster state.

High Availability: While single-instance setups suffice for many K3s deployments, critical production environments benefit from high availability configurations with multiple Prometheus replicas, federation, and persistent storage solutions supported by K3s.

Automation and GitOps: Manage configuration files and manifests declaratively via GitOps workflows. Utilize Helm charts or Kustomize overlays tailored for K3s to deploy and maintain Prometheus and Grafana with version control and seamless upgrades.

Instrumentation Hygiene: Maintain consistent metric naming conventions, labeling strategies, and avoid cardinality explosion from high-label-count metrics, which degrade Prometheus performance.

7.3. Container and Cluster Logging

In Kubernetes environments such as K3s, managing logs efficiently is critical to ensuring observability, debugging, and performance analysis. Logging in lightweight Kubernetes distributions presents unique challenges due to resource constraints and the distributed nature of workloads. This section presents detailed approaches to centralized and distributed logging within K3s, focusing on leveraging sidecar containers, log shippers like Fluentd and Logstash, and log aggregation solutions. It also examines storage considerations tied to log data management and outlines effective troubleshooting workflows.

K3s, designed for edge and resource-limited environments, still supports comprehensive logging architectures by combining native Kubernetes features with external tools. Logs can be broadly classified into container-level logs and cluster-level logs. Container logs capture standard output and error streams from individual pods, while cluster logs include control plane components, system daemons, and networking layers.

Sidecar Pattern for Container-Level Logging

One prevalent approach to container-level log collection in K3s is the sidecar pattern. This involves deploying an auxiliary container alongside the main application container within the same pod. The sidecar container is dedicated to log collection, processing, and forwarding, decoupling log management concerns from business logic.

Typically, the sidecar container mounts shared volumes or accesses the container runtime's log files (usually stored in `/var/log/containers/` or `/var/log/pods/`) to collect log entries. By isolating the log shipper into a sidecar, resource allocation can be adjusted independently, allowing for tailored configurations such as buffering size or retry policies without impacting the application container.

This pattern enhances reliability: if the log shipper encounters issues, it can be restarted without affecting the application container. Moreover, local processing like log transformation, filtering, and metadata enrichment can occur within the sidecar before forwarding.

Log Shippers: Fluentd and Logstash

Log shippers aggregate and forward logs from multiple sources to centralized storage or analysis platforms. Fluentd and Logstash are mature, widely adopted log shippers compatible with K3s deployments due to their flexible plugin architectures.

Fluentd is a lightweight daemon suitable for edge devices, making it a natural fit for K3s. It supports input plugins to tail container logs or receive syslog data, output plugins to forward logs to Elasticsearch, Kafka, or cloud logging services, and filter plugins for parsing and formatting. Fluentd's buffering and retry mechanisms provide resilience in scenarios with intermittent connectivity or backend downtime.

Fluentd typically runs as a DaemonSet in the cluster, ensuring every node runs one log collector instance. It gathers logs from all pods on the node, processes them, and forwards the structured logs to centralized storage with minimal overhead.

Logstash is part of the Elastic Stack and excels in complex parsing, enrichment, or transformation scenarios. Although heavier in resource consumption compared to Fluentd, it is valuable where advanced processing like pattern matching or multi-stage pipelines are required. Logstash can be deployed similarly as a DaemonSet or as a dedicated logging backend receiving data via various input protocols.

Log Aggregation Platforms

Collected logs are often aggregated in platforms designed to store, index, and query large volumes of log data for operational insights.

Common solutions integrated with K3s include:

- **Elasticsearch**: Paired with Kibana, Elasticsearch enables full-text search and real-time visualization of logs. It forms the backend of the Elastic Stack, scalable from single-node setups suitable for small clusters to distributed multi-node clusters.

- **Grafana Loki**: Designed for efficient log aggregation with minimal indexing, Loki stores logs in a compressed format indexed by labels, providing scalable yet cost-effective logging.

- **Cloud-Based Solutions**: Platforms such as AWS Cloud-Watch, Google Cloud Logging, or Azure Monitor can receive logs directly via Fluentd or Logstash outputs, offloading storage and management responsibilities from the cluster.

Log aggregation platforms benefit from structured and enriched log records, enabling quick filtering by pod names, namespaces, container IDs, and timestamps. Label-based querying enhances troubleshooting efficiency.

Storage and Retention Considerations

Logs are data-intensive, and improper handling can exhaust limited storage resources in edge deployments typical for K3s. Key considerations include:

- **Local Storage Limits**: Nodes may have constrained disk capacity, requiring log retention periods and buffer sizes to be carefully managed. Log rotation policies must ensure old log files are purged to prevent disk saturation.

- **Persistent Volumes**: When sidecar containers or DaemonSets write logs to persistent volumes, choosing storage classes with appropriate performance and durability is critical. Network-attached storage (NAS) or block storage providers can be used depending on cluster topology.

- **Compression and Archival**: Employing compression plugins during ingestion or configuring log shippers to archive older logs can reduce storage footprints.

- **Retention Policies**: Defining retention periods aligned with operational and compliance requirements balances log availability against storage costs. Many aggregation platforms support automatic index lifecycle management.

Selecting appropriate storage solutions also impacts log access latency and the feasibility of real-time troubleshooting.

Troubleshooting Workflows

A structured troubleshooting approach leveraging container and cluster logging is essential to rapidly identify and resolve issues:

- **Isolate the Scope**: Narrow down whether the issue originates at the container, pod, node, or cluster level.

- **Access Raw Logs**: Use `kubectl logs` or direct node access to retrieve logs from application containers or system components for initial diagnostics.

- **Leverage Aggregated Logs**: Query the centralized logging platform filtering by relevant labels-pod names, namespaces, timestamps, or error keywords-to identify widespread or correlated errors.

- **Analyze Sidecar Logs**: If using sidecar log collectors, inspect their logs to verify successful collection, parsing accuracy, and forwarding results.

- **Check Resource Metrics**: Cross-reference logging anomalies with resource metrics (CPU, memory, disk usage) collected via Prometheus or similar to detect resource exhaustion impacting logging.

- **Validate Log Shipper Health**: Investigate Fluentd or Logstash container status, buffer queues, and retry counts. Misconfigurations or network failures often impede log forwarding.

- **Adjust Configurations**: Update buffer sizes, rotation intervals, or parsing rules based on observed log patterns and volume.

Automated alerting integrated with logging platforms can expedite detection of anomalies, while maintaining logs accessible in readily queryable formats is vital for post-incident root cause analysis.

Effective container and cluster logging in K3s environments requires harmonizing architectural patterns such as sidecars, robust shipper implementations, scalable aggregation platforms, prudent storage planning, and disciplined troubleshooting. These combined practices ensure observability is maintained without overwhelming resource constraints, providing a foundation for resilient and manageable Kubernetes deployments.

7.4. Tracing and Distributed Context

Distributed tracing is indispensable for the observability of microservices architectures, particularly in lightweight Kubernetes distributions such as K3s. By capturing the propagation of requests as they traverse multiple services and infrastructure components, distributed tracing illuminates the often opaque interactions within a distributed system. This section delves into the practical implementation of distributed tracing using tools such as Jaeger and OpenTelemetry, emphasizing traffic correlation, context propagation, and the diagnosis of performance bottlenecks and errors across microservices deployed in K3s environments.

At the core of distributed tracing is the concept of *trace context*, a data structure propagated along with each request to represent the lineage of calls. This context comprises a *trace ID*, which uniquely identifies the entire transaction, and one or more *span IDs*, which denote specific operations or service spans within that transaction. Each span records timing information, metadata, and optionally logs or tags related to the operation it represents. Through context propagation, this trace context is transmitted across process boundaries, enabling the construction of a comprehensive end-to-end trace.

Implementation in K3s adheres to the same principles as in full-scale Kubernetes, with added attention to resource limitations and lightweight tooling compatibility. OpenTelemetry serves as an ideal vendor-neutral instrumentation framework, providing APIs and SDKs for generating traces and exporting them to backends such as Jaeger. Integrating OpenTelemetry within microservices instruments code paths to create spans and manages context propagation automatically via interceptors or middleware.

Context propagation occurs primarily through HTTP headers or messaging protocols. The OpenTelemetry specification defines the `traceparent` and `tracestate` headers (part of W3C Trace Context) to carry trace context in a standardized fashion. When a client initiates a request, it generates a new trace ID and span ID. Each downstream call then extracts, updates, and propagates this context, ensuring the trace identities' continuity across services.

Consider an example of context propagation using OpenTelemetry in a typical HTTP request handler in a Go microservice:

```
func handler(w http.ResponseWriter, r *http.Request) {
    ctx := r.Context()
    tracer := otel.Tracer("example-service")

    ctx, span := tracer.Start(ctx, "handleRequest")
    defer span.End()

    // Extract trace context from incoming request
    // Propagate context downstream with outgoing HTTP requests
    req, _ := http.NewRequestWithContext(ctx, "GET", "http://
     downstream-service/api", nil)
    client := http.Client{}
```

```
resp, err := client.Do(req)
if err != nil {
    span.RecordError(err)
    span.SetStatus(codes.Error, err.Error())
    http.Error(w, err.Error(), http.StatusInternalServerError
)
    return
}
defer resp.Body.Close()

w.WriteHeader(resp.StatusCode)
}
```

The embedded ctx contains an active span, implicitly transmitted in outbound requests via HTTP headers. OpenTelemetry's instrumentation libraries for HTTP clients and servers automatically marshal and unmarshal trace context, reducing manual handling and human error.

Jaeger acts as a scalable, production-ready tracing backend that collects, stores, and visualizes traces received from instrumented services. Installable within K3s either as a dedicated pod via Helm charts or as a sidecar agent, Jaeger aggregates spans and allows querying trace data in a web UI or via APIs for diagnostics.

Tracing data facilitates several critical diagnostic capabilities:

- **Performance Bottleneck Identification**: Spans record precise start and end times, enabling calculation of latencies for individual service calls. Visualizing the trace timeline across microservices uncovers latency hotspots, such as slow databases, overloaded services, or inefficient network hops.

- **Error and Exception Correlation**: Errors surfaced in spans are automatically correlated with their place in the trace, enabling operators to identify fault propagation chains. Tagging spans with error attributes and log entries enhances root cause analysis.

- **Traffic Flow Mapping**: Distributed tracing reconstructs the traffic paths in multi-service workflows, highlighting dependency graphs and invocation patterns. This is invaluable for understanding complex service topologies and the impact of changes within K3s clusters.

Context propagation through asynchronous messaging in event-driven K3s microservices requires additional instrumentation. Message brokers such as NATS or Kafka may not natively propagate HTTP headers, necessitating injection of trace context into message metadata or payload. OpenTelemetry provides APIs to extract and inject context into message carriers, preserving trace continuity across asynchronous boundaries.

An example of injecting and extracting trace context in Kafka messages is as follows:

```
func produceMessage(ctx context.Context, producer sarama.
    SyncProducer, topic string, msg []byte) error {
    tracer := otel.Tracer("example-producer")
    ctx, span := tracer.Start(ctx, "produceMessage")
    defer span.End()

    headers := make([]sarama.RecordHeader, 0)
    propagator := otel.GetTextMapPropagator()
    carrier := kafkaHeadersCarrier(headers)
    propagator.Inject(ctx, carrier)

    kafkaMsg := &sarama.ProducerMessage{
        Topic:   topic,
        Value:   sarama.ByteEncoder(msg),
        Headers: headers,
    }
    _, _, err := producer.SendMessage(kafkaMsg)
    if err != nil {
        span.RecordError(err)
        span.SetStatus(codes.Error, err.Error())
    }
    return err
}

func consumeMessage(ctx context.Context, msg *sarama.
    ConsumerMessage) {
    propagator := otel.GetTextMapPropagator()
    carrier := kafkaHeadersCarrier(msg.Headers)
    ctx = propagator.Extract(ctx, carrier)

    tracer := otel.Tracer("example-consumer")
    ctx, span := tracer.Start(ctx, "consumeMessage")
```

```
defer span.End()

// Process the message
}
```

Here, kafkaHeadersCarrier is an adapter implementing the TextMapCarrier interface for Sarama headers, enabling propagation of trace context.

In K3s environments constrained by compute resources, tracing overhead must be balanced against observability gains. Sampling strategies, configurable in OpenTelemetry SDKs and Jaeger agents, control the volume of trace data captured. Dynamic sampling can focus resources on high-error or high-latency scenarios, while excluding less critical traces during normal operation.

By combining automated instrumentation, standardized context propagation, and centralized collection with tools like OpenTelemetry and Jaeger, distributed tracing within K3s clusters delivers granular visibility into microservices interactions. This capability transforms opaque, distributed executions into interpretable traces, empowering developers and operators to swiftly pinpoint performance bottlenecks, trace failures, and optimize traffic flows in modern cloud-native applications.

7.5. Remote Monitoring for Edge and Fleet Deployments

Managing the operational health, performance, and security of large-scale edge and fleet deployments introduces challenges fundamentally distinct from centralized data center monitoring. The inherent characteristics of edge environments-geographical distribution, resource constraints, intermittent network connectivity, and heterogeneous device capabilities-necessitate sophisticated monitoring strategies that accommodate these constraints while delivering actionable insights.

A critical design consideration lies in selecting between *push-based* and *pull-based* telemetry data collection paradigms. In *pull-based* models, a central monitoring server periodically queries edge devices or clusters to retrieve status and metrics. While this approach simplifies central orchestration and ensures up-to-date data on demand, it may overwhelm limited bandwidth connections and is vulnerable to transient outages, making data collection unreliable when connectivity drops. Conversely, *push-based* systems delegate responsibility to edge devices to proactively transmit telemetry data when available. This model fosters scalability and resilience, as devices buffer data locally during offline periods and transmit asynchronously, reducing central server load and network congestion.

However, push-based collection presents challenges in controlling data flows and potentially imposing overhead on constrained edge nodes. To harmonize these concerns, hybrid mechanisms are often employed. For example, devices push high-priority alerts and summarized statistics, while the central system pulls detailed diagnostic data on-demand when connectivity and operational conditions permit. This selective instrumentation optimizes bandwidth usage and balances real-time responsiveness with data richness.

Aggregation nodes serve as pivotal intermediaries in remote monitoring architectures, positioned strategically to localize telemetry data preprocessing, filtering, and enrichment before forwarding to cloud or central repositories. In geographically dispersed fleets, deploying regional aggregation points reduces latency, lowers upstream data volumes, and enables early detection of anomalies through local correlation. Such nodes often possess more computational resources than edge devices, permitting execution of lightweight analytics, event deduplication, and security validations. Additionally, aggregation nodes provide resiliency by buffering data streams during network interruptions and enabling retransmission once connectivity is restored, preserving data integrity and continuity.

Architecting dashboards for operational visibility over distributed deployments demands careful consideration to consolidate heterogeneous data streams into coherent, actionable visualizations. Cloud-based dashboards offer centralized control planes with scalable storage and compute capabilities, facilitating long-term trend analysis, cross-site correlations, and integration with enterprise alerting systems. Edge-based dashboards complement this by providing localized, near-real-time status views tailored for on-site operators, capable of functioning autonomously during network outages.

Effective dashboard design incorporates multi-layered views that span granular device metrics (CPU, memory, sensor readings), cluster-level health indicators (node availability, network latency), and fleet-wide performance summaries (deployment status, anomaly rates). Employing adaptive data summarization techniques, such as data roll-ups and dimensionality reduction, ensures responsiveness despite large-scale data volumes. Integrating machine learning inference results directly into dashboards enables predictive maintenance and automated alerting, transforming raw data into prognostic insights.

Security considerations are paramount when exposing edge and fleet telemetry to central dashboards. Employing role-based access controls, encrypting data in transit and at rest, and maintaining audit trails ensure that sensitive operational data remains protected against unauthorized access and tampering. Furthermore, incorporating anomaly detection not only on performance metrics but also on monitoring data streams themselves can identify potential compromises or misconfigurations early.

In deployments characterized by intermittent or constrained connectivity, prioritization of telemetry data must be dynamic and context-aware. Critical system faults and security breaches warrant immediate transmission, whereas routine metrics can be batched and uploaded during off-peak periods or when bandwidth permits. Such intelligent throttling mechanisms reduce network strain and optimize storage utilization without sacrificing situational awareness.

Remote monitoring for edge and fleet deployments demands a robust, flexible architecture that harmonizes push and pull data collection methods, integrates intermediate aggregation nodes to localize processing and buffering, and delivers comprehensive dashboards designed for multi-scale visibility. This approach ensures reliable, scalable operational intelligence that overcomes the constraints imposed by distributed, intermittently connected environments, empowering operators to maintain system health and security with confidence.

7.6. Autoscaling and Resource Management

Efficient autoscaling and resource management in K3s, a lightweight Kubernetes distribution optimized for edge and IoT environments, necessitate careful configuration of Kubernetes primitives such as the Horizontal Pod Autoscaler (HPA). Unlike conventional, centralized cloud deployments, edge and IoT scenarios impose specific constraints including limited computational resources, network variability, and intermittent connectivity. These factors compel a nuanced approach to scaling policies and resource allocation.

The Horizontal Pod Autoscaler dynamically adjusts the number of pod replicas in a workload based on observed metrics, most commonly CPU or memory utilization, but also custom metrics if configured. In K3s, autoscaling is enabled by deploying the metrics-server or compatible adapters to aggregate resource metrics from nodes and pods. The HPA controller then periodically queries these metrics and alters replica counts to maintain desired performance levels.

A representative HPA manifest tailored to an edge workload might appear as follows:

```
apiVersion: autoscaling/v2
kind: HorizontalPodAutoscaler
metadata:
  name: edge-app-hpa
spec:
  scaleTargetRef:
    apiVersion: apps/v1
    kind: Deployment
    name: edge-app
  minReplicas: 1
  maxReplicas: 5
  metrics:
  - type: Resource
    resource:
      name: cpu
      target:
        type: Utilization
        averageUtilization: 60
```

This configuration maintains a minimum of one pod and scales up to five, targeting an average CPU utilization of 60%. However, in environments where resource availability fluctuates or is severely constrained, direct reliance on standard HPA configurations can lead to suboptimal scaling actions, such as overshooting CPU requests or oscillations in pod counts triggered by transient load spikes.

To address these challenges, scaling policies must be refined with an awareness of underlying physical constraints. For instance, appropriate value ranges for `minReplicas` and `maxReplicas` prevent resource exhaustion on edge devices. Additionally, the use of the `--horizontal-pod-autoscaler-upscale-delay` and `--horizontal-pod-autoscaler-downscale-delay` flags in K3s's controller manager allows tuning of the sensitivity and responsiveness of scaling decisions, thereby mitigating pod churn and ensuring system stability.

Beyond CPU and memory utilization, custom metrics provide the flexibility to scale based on application-specific indicators such as sensor data rates, message queue lengths, or network latency. Integration of Prometheus and custom exporters in K3s clusters enables the HPA to leverage these metrics via the Kubernetes External Metrics API. This is critical in IoT scenarios where workload intensity correlates more directly with event rates or context-aware triggers rather than traditional resource consumption patterns.

Resource requests and limits form another vital aspect of resource management that directly influence autoscaling outcomes. Correctly specified requests enable the Kubernetes scheduler to place pods efficiently given the node capacities, while limits prevent any pod from monopolizing shared resources and degrading cluster stability. Due to constrained memory and CPU on edge nodes, conservative and empirically validated resource allocations are essential. Over-provisioning leads to resource contention, whereas under-provisioning risks throttling performance and causing frequent pod evictions.

In addition to HPA, Vertical Pod Autoscaler (VPA) can be used cautiously in edge deployments to adjust the resource requests for individual pods over time. However, VPA and HPA should not be used simultaneously on the same workload due to conflicting update strategies. Thus, workload profiling and resource usage history are invaluable for tuning both horizontal and vertical scaling to balance responsiveness and resource efficiency.

Network-related constraints in edge environments influence autoscaling strategies as well. Latency-sensitive applications may benefit from maintaining warm standby pods through minimum replica counts rather than aggressive scaling to zero or near-zero replicas. Scaling down too aggressively can incur significant startup delays and packet loss in tightly coupled IoT systems.

The orchestration of autoscaling in K3s for edge and IoT contexts demands a harmonization of Kubernetes scaling primitives with resource-aware policies. Practical deployment considerations include tuning HPA thresholds and delays, leveraging custom metrics for context-aware scaling, stringent resource requests and limits aligned to device capabilities, and acknowledging network and latency implications. This integrated approach ensures workloads remain resilient, performant, and resource-efficient within the unique constraints of decentralized edge architectures.

Chapter 8

Scaling, Multi-Cluster, and Lifecycle Operations

From a single node to fleet-wide orchestration, this chapter reveals how K3s adapts to the evolving needs of dynamic infrastructures. Explore seamless scaling, multi-cluster federation, and the critical lifecycle techniques that sustain clusters through upgrades, failures, and decommissioning — all tailored to match the agility and constraints of lightweight deployments.

8.1. Cluster Expansion and Dynamic Node Management

Managing node lifecycle events within active K3s clusters involves intricate coordination between cluster state, workload scheduling, and node resource metrics to ensure minimal disruption and optimal performance. This section expands on the processes for adding, removing, and upgrading nodes, integrating core concepts of node discovery, continuous health monitoring, and methods for live cluster resizing.

Node Addition and Discovery Mechanisms

In K3s, node addition begins with bootstrapping the new node to join the cluster control plane. This process relies on effective node discovery protocols, typically based on a shared cluster token or certificate authority mechanism for secure authentication. Nodes intended for integration must be preconfigured with the service URL of the cluster and the shared token to participate in the joining handshake.

Upon node startup, the K3s agent initiates communication with the server, verifying node identity and readiness. The agent then registers the node's metadata, including its labels, capacity, and taints, enabling the Kubernetes scheduler to recognize and efficiently allocate pods. The Kubernetes API server maintains an updated list of nodes, reflecting these new additions.

This automated discovery process leverages the Kubernetes Control Plane's node watcher mechanism, which listens for node-related events and triggers appropriate reconciliations. Internally, the K3s server employs a lightweight variant of the kubelet to continuously update node status, ensuring prompt reflection of changes within the cluster state database (etcd or embedded SQLite).

Node Health Checks and Continuous Monitoring

Sustained cluster stability demands rigorous node health validation, executed through a combination of liveness probes and readiness checks. The K3s control plane continuously monitors nodes via heartbeats transmitted from kubelet processes on each node at regular intervals (default 10 seconds). Loss of heartbeat triggers node status changes to NotReady, prompting the scheduler to take remedial action such as pod eviction or rescheduling.

Health checks involve multiple dimensions:

- **Node Conditions:** These include network availability, disk pressure, memory pressure, and PID pressure states, each reported through node status objects.

- **Pod Health:** Readiness and liveness probes configured per pod allow preemptive exclusion of nodes hosting unhealthy pods from receiving new workload assignments.

- **Resource Usage Metrics:** Resource consumption metrics gathered via lightweight monitoring agents (e.g., metrics-server) guide decisions about node scalability and pod placement.

The control plane reconciles these signals to maintain high availability, optimizing cluster resilience through proactive workload migration or node replacement.

Node Removal and Draining Procedures

Node removal necessitates careful orchestration to avoid workload disruption and prevent data loss. K3s supports cordoning and draining nodes:

- **Cordoning:** Marks the node as unschedulable, preventing new pods from being assigned while allowing existing pods to continue running.

- **Draining:** Initiates eviction of all pods, respecting graceful termination periods and ensuring graceful shutdown of stateful applications.

Consider the following sequence to safely remove a node:

```
kubectl cordon <node_name>
kubectl drain <node_name> --ignore-daemonsets --delete-emptydir-
    data
kubectl delete node <node_name>
```

Drain operations explicitly handle daemonsets and local storage implications. The flag `--ignore-daemonsets` allows daemonset-managed pods to remain, while `--delete-emptydir-data` marks ephemeral storage for cleaning. Following successful eviction and state synchronization, the node can be removed from the cluster metadata safely.

Live Node Upgrades and Version Management

Upgrading nodes in K3s clusters involves applying new K3s agent versions without disrupting existing workloads or cluster control operations. Coordinated rolling upgrades leverage Kubernetes' built-in rollout and drain capabilities alongside K3s-specific agent management commands:

- Upgrade the control plane components first to ensure compatibility and new API features.

- Sequentially upgrade worker nodes by draining each node, upgrading the agent software, and then uncordoning.

Automated upgrade scripts typically perform the following:

```
kubectl drain <node_name> --ignore-daemonsets --delete-emptydir-
    data
# Upgrade K3s agent on the node, e.g., via package manager or
    installation script
systemctl restart k3s-agent
kubectl uncordon <node_name>
```

This approach maintains service continuity: pods are rescheduled on healthy nodes during upgrade, ensuring uninterrupted workload delivery.

Strategies for Live Resizing and Dynamic Scaling

Dynamic resizing-adding or removing capacity in response to workload demands-relies on a set of strategies to minimize impact:

- **Horizontal Pod Autoscaling (HPA) Integration:** K3s

clusters integrate seamlessly with HPA controllers, which adjust pod replicas based on metrics, necessitating corresponding node capacity adjustments.

- **Cluster Autoscaler Compatibility:** Although K3s does not supply a native autoscaler, it is compatible with the Kubernetes Cluster Autoscaler, which interfaces with cloud or physical infrastructure providers to automate node management based on pod scheduling failures or over-provisioning.

- **Graceful Pod Eviction and Rescheduling:** During node removal or scaling down, workload is redistributed using Kubernetes rescheduling policies, prioritizing affinity, anti-affinity, and taints/tolerations.

- **Pre-drain Readiness Checks:** These validate that alternative nodes have sufficient capacity to absorb workloads before nodes are removed, ensuring seamless failover.

K3s' lightweight architecture allows rapid node addition and removal, making it well-suited for environments that demand elastic scaling while maintaining operational integrity.

Summary of Best Practices

Operational excellence in dynamic node management within K3s clusters is achieved through:

- Ensuring secure and authenticated node discovery through shared tokens or certificates.

- Implementing continuous health checks and resource monitoring to prevent silent failures.

- Employing cordon and drain procedures for safe node removal.

- Conducting rolling upgrades using controlled node draining and agent restarts.

- Leveraging Kubernetes native autoscaling frameworks to enable automated cluster resizing.

The integration of these processes enables K3s clusters to evolve flexibly with application demands while safeguarding workload availability and consistency.

8.2. Multi-Cluster Orchestration and Federation

The management of multiple K3s clusters introduces complexities beyond those encountered in single-cluster environments, necessitating sophisticated orchestration and federation strategies to achieve scalable, resilient, and consistent operation across distributed infrastructure. The fundamental challenge lies in unifying control over disparate K3s clusters while preserving autonomy, optimizing resource utilization, and enabling workload mobility without sacrificing security or operational simplicity.

Federated control planes constitute a primary approach for multi-cluster management, enabling the aggregation of cluster state and policy automation across heterogeneous K3s deployments. A federation layer typically comprises a central controller that synchronizes Kubernetes API objects-such as Namespaces, Deployments, and Services-across clusters, ensuring consistent configuration and workload orchestration. Patterns such as cluster-aware controllers or the Kubernetes Cluster API Federation (KubeFed) facilitate declarative multi-cluster resource management.

State reconciliation in federated systems demands careful consideration of object lifecycle semantics and conflict resolution. For example, propagating resource quotas and Role-Based Access Control (RBAC) policies from a centralized authority requires bidirectional synchronization to handle local overrides and resolve inconsistencies. The federation control plane often utilizes custom resource definitions (CRDs) to extend Kubernetes capabilities, providing abstractions for "federated" resources that map onto underlying cluster-specific objects.

Centralized policy enforcement is essential for effective governance in multi-cluster environments. Tools such as Open Policy Agent (OPA) and Gatekeeper enable the definition of cluster-agnostic policies that can be applied consistently across K3s clusters. These policies cover a broad spectrum-from security baselines and resource quotas to network policies and admission controls-ensuring compliance without manual drift.

Centralized policy enforcement is typically implemented via admission webhooks integrated into each K3s API server, configured to consult a centralized policy repository. Such architecture enables the propagation of policy updates in near real-time and provides auditability across clusters. When integrated into federated control planes, it establishes a holistic governance model enforcing organizational policies seamlessly and uniformly.

Workload portability and synchronization underpin strategies for load balancing, geo-distribution, and hybrid-cloud deployment. Abstracting application manifests as cluster-agnostic Helm charts or Kubernetes Operators enables deployment automation irrespective of the underlying environment. Synchronization of persistent state, especially for stateful workloads, requires specialized approaches such as distributed storage solutions (e.g., Ceph, Longhorn) or data replication techniques ensuring data consistency across nodes and clusters.

Service discovery mechanisms in federated setups often employ DNS-based routing or service mesh technologies like Istio and Linkerd to enable cross-cluster communication and failover. These solutions provide granular traffic control-including retry logic and circuit breaking-thus enhancing availability and performance amid cluster failures or network partitions.

Failover and resilience across multiple K3s clusters demand fault-tolerant architectures that accommodate failover at both the control plane and data plane layers. Control plane failover strategies involve replicating key components (API servers, controllers) with consensus mechanisms such as etcd clustering or external datastore backends managed by distributed databases.

Workload failover can be realized via cluster-aware schedulers or controllers that detect node or cluster outages and reassign pods accordingly. Integration with continuous health monitoring systems and alerting enables automated remediation. Load balancers with geo-aware routing direct user traffic to the nearest healthy cluster, minimizing latency while ensuring continuity.

Geo-distribution and hybrid-cloud patterns serve both regulatory compliance and latency optimization objectives by placing clusters in proximity to users or data sources. This distribution introduces network variability and potential partitioning, which federated orchestration must mitigate through eventual consistency models and conflict resolution policies.

Hybrid-cloud architectures extend this paradigm by combining on-premises K3s clusters with public cloud instances. Workload portability in hybrid-cloud setups is facilitated by container registries supporting multi-region replication and infrastructure as code (IaC) templates that abstract environment differences. Networking across hybrid-cloud clusters often employs VPNs, software-defined WANs (SD-WAN), or cloud provider interconnects to enable secure, seamless communication.

Hybrid setups benefit from multi-cluster ingress controllers and federated service meshes to handle traffic routing transparently, enabling dynamic scaling and failover across cloud boundaries. Cloud-native observability tools aggregate metrics and logs across these heterogeneous environments, facilitating unified operational visibility and troubleshooting.

The orchestration of multiple K3s clusters can be conceptualized along three intersecting vectors: control plane federation, policy governance, and workload mobility. Each vector demands specialized mechanisms-ranging from federated API synchronization to centralized policy engines and resilient multi-cluster networking. Architectures must embrace eventual consistency, multi-tenancy isolation, and secure communication channels to balance automation with operational control.

Central orchestration reduces management overhead, while enabling rapid failover and dynamic workload placement fosters system resilience and performance across geo-distributed or hybrid-cloud deployments. Custom tooling combined with leveraging upstream Kubernetes federation projects helps tailor solutions specific to organizational objectives, cluster scale, and infrastructure diversity.

In practice, successful multi-cluster orchestration with K3s builds upon coordinated configuration management, robust policy frameworks, and advanced networking infrastructures. This integrated approach transforms multi-cluster landscapes from isolated silos into cohesive, agile platforms capable of supporting modern, distributed cloud-native applications.

8.3. Rollout, Rollback, and Zero Downtime Strategies

K3s, a lightweight Kubernetes distribution optimized for edge and resource-constrained environments, inherits Kubernetes' fundamental deployment methodologies while incorporating optimizations suited to its streamlined architecture. Achieving application and infrastructure updates with zero or minimal downtime in K3s environments necessitates a nuanced application of Kubernetes-native concepts adapted to the constraints and features unique to K3s nodes and clusters.

Phased rollout techniques in K3s utilize the native Kubernetes Deployment resource's rolling update strategy, balancing availability with progressive exposure to new code. The Deployment controller incrementally updates pods in a replicaset, maintaining the desired number of available pods during the process. K3s' reduced resource overhead and simplified components improve update latency, which is critical in edge scenarios where network conditions and compute resources fluctuate.

To implement phased rollouts in K3s, define the Deployment spec with the `strategy` field set to `RollingUpdate`, specifying parameters such as `maxSurge` and `maxUnavailable`. These parameters regulate how aggressively the cluster replaces pods:

```
apiVersion: apps/v1
kind: Deployment
metadata:
  name: example-service
spec:
  replicas: 5
  strategy:
    type: RollingUpdate
    rollingUpdate:
      maxSurge: 1
      maxUnavailable: 0
  template:
    metadata:
      labels:
        app: example
    spec:
      containers:
      - name: example-container
        image: example/image:latest
```

This configuration ensures that up to one additional pod can be created during the update, allowing uninterrupted service availability while gradually replacing existing pods. Given the constrained resources typical of K3s clusters, careful tuning of these values prevents resource saturation and ensures stability.

Canary deployments, an advanced form of phased rollout, route only a small subset of traffic to the new version while the majority continues to access the stable version. This approach facilitates direct comparison and performance monitoring under real user conditions. Although Kubernetes does not natively provide traffic routing capabilities for canary deployments, K3s' compatibility with service mesh solutions or ingress controllers that support traffic splitting enables effective canary strategies.

In K3s environments, Istio or Linkerd can be deployed with minimized resource profiles, or lightweight ingress controllers such as Traefik, which natively supports weighted routing rules, may be preferred. Configuring weighted routing between two Deployment replicasets allows the canary subset to be incrementally increased.

An example using Traefik's Kubernetes IngressRoute might resemble:

```
apiVersion: traefik.containo.us/v1alpha1
kind: IngressRoute
metadata:
  name: example-canary
spec:
  routes:
  - kind: Rule
    match: Host(`service.example.com`)
    services:
    - name: example-stable
      port: 80
      weight: 90
    - name: example-canary
      port: 80
      weight: 10
```

This arrangement directs 10% of user requests to the canary version pods, enabling performance validation before wider rollout. K3s' minimal footprint mitigates overhead when deploying such auxiliary components, making this practical even on edge nodes.

Rollback strategies are integral to maintaining zero downtime during failures. K3s leverages Kubernetes' atomic update semantics and revision histories to provide rollback capabilities. The Deployment resource retains prior replicaset configurations, allowing a rollback command to revert to a known stable state.

Executing:

```
kubectl rollout undo deployment/example-service
```

reinstates the previous Deployment revision. Robust rollback depends on monitoring and readiness probes to detect failures promptly, enabling automated or operator-driven interventions. K3s' rapid convergence speeds, via lightweight controllers and optimized control plane components, reduce the window of failure exposure.

For stateful applications or complex topologies, rollback strategies must be augmented with data consistency guarantees, such as using persistent volume snapshots or versioned database schemas, beyond the scope of Deployment rollbacks. K3s clusters often operate with local storage drivers optimized for edge environments, necessitating tailored data protection mechanisms integrated with rollback actions.

K3s' design choices influence rollout and rollback practices. The single binary architecture and embedded SQLite datastore (or external databases in HA setups) streamline control plane operations but demand careful HA planning to avoid single points of failure during updates.

To maintain zero downtime during control plane upgrades-a foundational element for application availability-K3s supports running server nodes in HA configurations with embedded or external datastore backends. Rolling upgrades of server nodes can be orchestrated sequentially with draining and cordoning, preventing disruption to the cluster state and worker node scheduling.

Worker nodes benefit from lightweight kubelets and streamlined networking (via Flannel or alternatives), reducing pod startup times and improving rolling update performance. Leveraging taints and tolerations allows selective pod migration, aiding in phased rollouts or rollbacks where resource balancing is critical.

Implementing zero downtime deployment cycles in K3s

environments is enhanced by integrating with continuous delivery pipelines and observability tools. Kubernetes-native frameworks such as Argo Rollouts facilitate declarative canary and blue-green deployment patterns with built-in metric analysis and automated promotion or rollback decisions.

Although headless, K3s can accommodate Argo Rollouts and Prometheus exporters, provided appropriate resource allowances. Automation must respect K3s' edge constraints, scaling rollout batch sizes and traffic weights conservatively.

For monitoring deployment health, readiness and liveness probes remain pivotal. K3s nodes' resource constraints heighten the importance of fine-tuning probe intervals and thresholds to avoid false positives triggering premature rollbacks or downtime.

- Utilize the native `RollingUpdate` strategy with conservative `maxSurge` and `maxUnavailable` settings to maintain application availability within resource-limited K3s clusters.

- Deploy lightweight ingress controllers like Traefik for traffic weight distribution enabling canary deployments, adapting the traffic split incrementally based on real-time metrics.

- Rely on `kubectl rollout undo` and Kubernetes revision history for dependable rollback, supplemented by thorough readiness probes and observability.

- Plan control plane upgrades as rolling updates across server nodes in HA mode, preventing total cluster downtime.

- Integrate CI/CD tools capable of orchestrating phased deployment strategies tuned for the K3s operational profile.

Incorporation of these strategies within K3s clusters facilitates robust, zero downtime delivery workflows essential for edge and lightweight environments, balancing agility with reliability under constrained conditions.

8.4. Automated Upgrades and GitOps Workflow Integration

The automation of cluster upgrades and maintenance constitutes a critical aspect of modern Kubernetes operations, reducing manual intervention while increasing reliability and consistency. Integrating these automated processes within GitOps workflows further enhances operational transparency and control by leveraging declarative configurations as the single source of truth. This section dissects the tooling and practices essential for achieving orchestrated upgrades, paying particular attention to the synergy between cluster lifecycle automation, GitOps principles, and continuous integration/continuous deployment (CI/CD) pipelines using industry-leading tools such as ArgoCD and Flux.

Cluster upgrades involve the controlled update of Kubernetes control planes and worker nodes, often accompanied by updates to associated infrastructure components, network plugins, and workload manifests. To orchestrate these upgrades with minimal downtime, automation tools must support version management, dependency resolution, and rollback strategies. Operating within a GitOps framework mandates that upgrade manifests and strategies be defined, tested, and version-controlled declaratively within Git repositories, ensuring auditability and traceability.

ArgoCD and Flux exemplify the most mature GitOps operators that reconcile desired cluster state defined in Git with the live cluster state. These tools are extended to manage not only application deployments but also cluster-wide configuration and versioning, enabling automated cluster upgrades when combined with appropriate operators or scripts.

ArgoCD-based Upgrade Automation

ArgoCD relies on a declarative approach by continuously monitoring Git repositories and applying changes to Kubernetes resources.

To integrate cluster upgrade workflows, a common pattern involves defining Kubernetes manifests for upgrade controllers or operators as part of the Git repository. For example, the Kubernetes Cluster API (CAPI) manifests used for infrastructure lifecycle management can be managed within ArgoCD applications.

Upgrades can be triggered by updating the Git repository with new version manifests or configuration changes, which ArgoCD then reconciles automatically. To safely perform upgrades, manifests typically include canary rollout strategies or pause hooks. ArgoCD's support for hooks allows execution of pre-sync and post-sync steps such as backing up cluster state, running health checks, or draining nodes before an upgrade is applied.

Integration with CI/CD pipelines enables automation of manifest generation and validation. A typical workflow commits changes to a dedicated upgrade branch or pull request, where a pipeline triggers CI validation-executing unit tests, integration tests, and policy checks. Upon success, these changes are merged into the main branch, triggering ArgoCD to perform the upgrade. This approach ensures compliance and operational safety through progressive verification.

Flux-based Upgrade Management

Flux operates with a similar declarative reconciliation loop, tailored with `GitRepository`, `Kustomization`, and `HelmRepository` resources that describe the desired state. Cluster upgrades via Flux usually involve automating changes to Helm chart versions or Kustomize overlays representing cluster components.

Flux's built-in automation controllers can watch for new Helm chart releases or external version updates, automatically creating pull requests to update the Git repository. This automation supports seamless upgrade rollouts after human or automated approvals. Integration with notification systems allows operators to receive alerts for available upgrades, audit change proposals, and intervene if needed.

Flux's capability to manage source control branch synchronization enables staged promotion of upgrade artifacts through environments (e.g., dev, staging, production). This aligns with GitOps best practices by enforcing strict promotion gates and automated validations at each stage.

CI/CD Pipelines in Support of Upgrade Workflows

CI/CD pipelines complement ArgoCD and Flux by generating, validating, and publishing configuration changes that define cluster upgrades. Common tasks automated in pipelines include:

- **Version Bumping and Manifest Generation:** Using scripts or tools like Kustomize, Helm, or Helmfile, pipelines update version references and regenerate manifests in Git repositories.

- **Testing and Validation:** Static analysis tools (e.g., kubeval, conftest), integration test suites, and policy frameworks (e.g., Open Policy Agent) run prior to merge approval.

- **Security Scanning:** Containers and dependency chain scanning ensures no vulnerabilities propagate during upgrades.

- **Automated Pull Request Creation:** Pipelines may create upgrade proposals as pull requests for review, leveraging GitOps pull request automation patterns.

This integration allows for rapid iteration of upgrade manifests with clear evidence of compliance and stability before production rollout, effectively reducing operational risk.

Challenges and Best Practices

While GitOps-driven automated upgrades significantly improve cluster manageability, orchestrating complex multi-component upgrades requires classifying resources by upgrade impact and dependencies to avoid cascading failures. This may involve customizing operator hooks or applying staged rollout strategies controlled via GitOps manifests.

Observability tools integrated within GitOps workflows provide diagnostic information during upgrades, increasing confidence in automated rollbacks. Furthermore, operators must enforce reconciliation intervals consistent with upgrade windows and incorporate health probes to detect anomalies promptly.

Security considerations include managing the credential lifecycle for pipeline runners, GitOps operators, and cloud APIs to grant only the needed privileges for upgrades, minimizing the blast radius of potential misconfigurations.

Case Study: Automated CAPI Cluster Upgrades via ArgoCD

Consider a scenario utilizing the Cluster API (CAPI) for managing Kubernetes clusters declaratively. Infrastructure manifests, cluster template versions, and control plane machine deployments are stored in a Git repository tracked by ArgoCD. A CI pipeline detects new upstream Kubernetes releases and updates the cluster template manifests to a target version.

After running conformance and integration tests in a staging environment, the changes merge into the production branch. ArgoCD reconciles the manifests and initiates the rolling upgrade of machines by sequentially upgrading control plane nodes and worker nodes. Known best practices such as machine health checks and machine set scaling policies ensure no downtime during upgrade. Pre- and post-sync hooks in ArgoCD enable backup and validation steps, closing the automation loop with full auditability.

```
apiVersion: batch/v1
kind: Job
metadata:
  name: backup-before-upgrade
  annotations:
```

```
      argocd.argoproj.io/hook: PreSync
 spec:
   template:
     spec:
       containers:
       - name: backup
         image: cluster-backup:latest
         command: ["backup-script.sh"]
         restartPolicy: OnFailure
```

```
$ kubectl get jobs
NAME                     COMPLETIONS   DURATION   AGE
backup-before-upgrade    1/1              12s      1m
```

GitOps-driven automation harmonizes cluster lifecycle management with enterprise-grade software engineering practices, elevating upgrade procedures from error-prone manual tasks to codified, repeatable, and observable processes that scale across infrastructures and teams. This tightly integrated approach is indispensable for organizations aiming to maintain robust Kubernetes environments in dynamic production settings.

8.5. Backup, Restore, and Disaster Recovery Operations

Effective operational recovery in modern distributed systems necessitates meticulously designed playbooks that encompass scheduled and on-demand backups, state restoration, and continuous testing of disaster recovery (DR) readiness. This is especially critical in environments with both single and multiple clusters, where data consistency, availability, and rapid recovery are paramount.

Backup Strategies: Scheduled and On-Demand

Backups serve as the foundational element of disaster recovery, safeguarding critical system state and data against failures. Scheduled backups are automated, recurring operations triggered at predetermined intervals-hourly, daily, or weekly-depending on the criticality of the data and the acceptable recovery point objective (RPO). These backups ensure a consistent archival of system state with minimal human intervention, reducing operational risk.

On-demand backups complement scheduled operations by providing ad hoc snapshots before risky operations such as major upgrades or configuration changes. These can be initiated manually or triggered by predefined events within an automation pipeline. The playbook must specify:

- The backup sources, including persistent storage volumes, configuration snapshots, and metadata stores.

- Consistency requirements, ensuring application quiescence or filesystem freeze when needed to capture a coherent state.

- Retention policies governing the lifespan and archival storage of backup artifacts.

- Security measures including encryption, access controls, and integrity verification.

A typical command for initiating an on-demand backup in a Kubernetes environment might involve leveraging native CSI snapshots and external backup tools, as shown below:

```
velero backup create pre-upgrade-backup --include-namespaces app-
    namespace --snapshot-volumes
```

The output confirms successful backup creation:

```
Backup request "pre-upgrade-backup" submitted successfully.
Run `velero backup describe pre-upgrade-backup` or `velero backup logs pre-up
grade-backup`
to check status.
```

State Restoration Procedures

Restoration workflows must address both granular and full-cluster recovery scenarios. Restoration operations reconstruct cluster states from backups to a defined recovery point while minimizing downtime and data loss. Key considerations in the playbook include:

- The scope of restoration: namespace-level, resource-level, or entire cluster.

- Order and dependency resolution, determining the correct sequence to restore critical components (e.g., etcd state, persistent volumes, CRDs, and application workloads).

- Validation steps post-restoration to verify consistency and application health.

- Rollback mechanisms in case restoration introduces unexpected issues.

In multi-cluster environments, state restoration must consider the orchestration of interdependent cluster states, often requiring federated control plane coordination. Below is a succinct example that demonstrates restoring a Velero backup:

```
velero restore create --from-backup pre-upgrade-backup
```

Monitoring progress and errors during restoration is equally critical:

```
Restore request "pre-upgrade-backup-restore" submitted successfully.
Run `velero restore describe pre-upgrade-backup-restore` or `velero restore l
ogs pre-upgrade-backup-restore`
to check status.
```

Testing Disaster Recovery Readiness

Robust disaster recovery planning mandates regular testing to verify the efficacy of backup and restoration processes. Testing simulates failure scenarios to validate recovery time objective (RTO) and RPO compliance. The playbook delineates multiple testing modalities:

- *Tabletop exercises*: cognitive walkthroughs to confirm procedural clarity among operations teams.

- *Automated failover drills*: scripted simulations that orchestrate partial or full failover to backup clusters or cloud regions.

- *Scheduled restores*: periodic restoration of backups into isolated environments to validate artifact integrity and process correctness.

Multi-cluster DR testing involves mimicking complex failure modes such as regional outages or network partitioning, ensuring federated clusters can failover seamlessly or recover independently without data loss.

Below is a schematic algorithm for an automated DR test routine, abstracted for a multi-cluster Kubernetes setup:

Algorithm 1 Automated Disaster Recovery Test for Multi-Cluster Setup

---

1: Trigger on-demand backup across all clusters:
2: **for all** clusters C in federation **do**
3:     $B_C \leftarrow$ createBackup(C)
4: **end for**
5: Deploy restoration environments isolated from production:
6: **for all** B_C **do**
7:     $R_C \leftarrow$ restoreBackup(B_C) in test namespace
8: **end for**
9: **for all** R_C **do**
10:     Run health checks and application smoke tests
11:     **if** any check fails **then**
12:         Report failure and halt test
13:     **end if**
14: **end for**
15: Remove restoration environments
16: Confirm no residual impact on live clusters

Operational Considerations and Best Practices

Integration of backup and recovery playbooks into CI/CD pipelines enhances agility and reduces manual errors. Advanced orchestration platforms provide webhook hooks and reconciliation loops to trigger backups automatically before deployment stages.

Consistency across clusters in multi-region deployments requires synchronization of backup schedules and preservation of backup metadata in centralized, immutable stores. Role-based access controls (RBAC) and audit logging reinforce security and compliance requirements.

Finally, backup storage architectures must incorporate high durability and geographic redundancy. Cloud-native object storage, combined with immutable snapshots, guard against ransomware and accidental deletion.

Disaster recovery playbooks become living documents that evolve with the infrastructure landscape, driven by operational metrics, incident postmortems, and evolving business continuity demands.

8.6. High Availability and Cross-Region/Edge Synchronization

Achieving high availability in distributed systems, particularly those spanning multiple regions and edge clusters, requires robust strategies to ensure continuous operation despite failures, network partitions, and varying latencies. The core challenge lies in maintaining a consistent global state and coordinated decision-making processes while minimizing service disruption. This involves the integration of consensus protocols, leader election mechanisms, and effective replication strategies tuned to the heterogeneity of distributed environments.

A fundamental principle in ensuring high availability and consistency under failures is the use of a *quorum-based* approach. A quorum is a subset of nodes whose agreement is sufficient to perform an operation safely, such as committing a transaction or electing a leader. By requiring a majority (or other carefully chosen threshold) of nodes to participate in decisions, the system can tolerate failures of minority subsets without risking state divergence. The most common quorum selection is the majority quorum, ensuring any two quorums intersect in at least one node, thereby supporting consistency guarantees.

High availability often mandates a *leader election* process to coordinate updates or manage metadata. Leader election algorithms like Paxos, Raft, and Zab implement state machine replication protocols designed to tolerate failures by electing a leader responsible for serializing state changes. The leader periodically sends heartbeats to assert its authority and prompt followers to replicate logs. If heartbeats are missed due to failure or network problems, a new leader election is triggered to restore consensus leadership. This process must be resilient to network partitions preventing split-brain scenarios where multiple leaders temporarily coexist, which could corrupt state.

When expanding the deployment beyond a single region to multiple geographically distributed regions or edge clusters, significant challenges arise related to high latency, network reliability, and partial visibility. *Cross-region synchronization* necessitates techniques that balance consistency, latency, and availability trade-offs often captured in the CAP theorem framework. Direct synchronous replication across wide-area networks incurs considerable latency; asynchronous or semi-synchronous replication techniques thus become indispensable in such scenarios.

Remote replication strategies encompass both *primary-secondary* and *multi-primary* models. In the primary-secondary model, all writes funnel through a single region that acts as the authoritative source. Secondary replicas asynchronously or semi-synchronously replicate changes to other regions or edge clusters to serve reads or provide failover support. This model simplifies consistency and leader election but may introduce read and write latency penalties for clients distant from the primary. Conversely, multi-primary (or multi-leader) approaches allow multiple regions to accept writes independently, requiring sophisticated conflict detection and resolution protocols, such as vector clocks or operational transformation, to manage divergent updates.

The systemic complexity of remote replication is compounded by the challenges of maintaining *state synchronization* among edge clusters. Edge environments frequently experience intermittent connectivity, limited bandwidth, and resource constraints. Consequently, replication protocols must handle partial updates, delayed synchronization, and conflict resolution gracefully. Techniques such as *log shipping*, delta-based updates, or Conflict-Free Replicated Data Types (CRDTs) provide mechanisms to propagate state changes efficiently and reconcile differences without central coordination.

Leader election in multi-region systems becomes more nuanced, as geographic partitioning can isolate subsets of nodes, each potentially considering itself eligible to lead. To mitigate these risks, algorithms can incorporate region-aware voting where quorums are constructed to ensure geographic diversity, preventing single-region domination and enabling continued operation when connectivity is compromised. Hybrid approaches combine strong consistency locally with eventual consistency across regions, enabling responsiveness and availability while reconverging global state over time.

The latency and fault tolerance requirements also influence the selection of consensus algorithms. For instance, Raft is often favored for its understandability and simplicity in moderate-scale regional clusters, whereas Paxos variants or Byzantine Fault Tolerant protocols may be employed in adversarial or highly unreliable environments. Furthermore, leader election timeouts and heartbeat intervals are typically configured with network delays and failure detection sensitivities tuned to the multi-region topology to avoid premature failovers or prolonged leadership uncertainty.

A critical factor in high availability design is the handling of network partitions, where communication failures may isolate regions or edge clusters. Systems employing quorums must ensure that only subsets possessing the quorum can continue processing writes, thereby preventing divergence. Stale or isolated replicas remain in read-only or disconnected modes until rejoining the quorum, at which point reconciliation occurs through log replay or state merge. The system's ability to detect partitions promptly and transition into a consistent operational state directly affects user-perceived availability.

Finally, security and data integrity during cross-region synchronization introduce additional considerations. Encryption for data in transit, authentication between clusters, and integrity validation mechanisms safeguard against unauthorized access and data corruption. Coordinating updates and access control across heterogeneous administrative domains requires well-architected identity and policy frameworks.

```
def initiateElection(currentTerm: Int, peers: List[Peer],
    electionTimeout: FiniteDuration): Future[Boolean] = {
  val votes = new AtomicInteger(1) // vote for self
  val quorum = (peers.size / 2) + 1

  val voteRequests = peers.map { peer =>
    peer.requestVote(currentTerm).map {
      case VoteGranted => votes.incrementAndGet()
      case _ => ()
    }
  }

  Future.sequence(voteRequests).map(_ =>
    votes.get() >= quorum
  ).recover {
    case _ => false
```

```
  }
}

def onElectionTimeout(): Unit = {
  currentTerm += 1
  state = Candidate
  val wonElection = await(initiateElection(currentTerm,
    regionPeers, electionTimeout))
  if (wonElection) {
    state = Leader
    sendHeartbeats()
  } else {
    state = Follower
  }
}
```

```
Output Example:
Peer A granted vote for term 5.
Peer B granted vote for term 5.
Peer C denied vote for term 5.
Votes received: 2 out of 3.
Node becomes leader for term 5.
```

The interplay of quorum techniques, leader election algorithms, and remote replication designs enables distributed systems to achieve high availability and consistent state synchronization across heterogeneous regional and edge deployments. Achieving an optimal balance requires careful consideration of network characteristics, failure modes, and application-specific correctness criteria.

8.7. Cluster Decommissioning and Secure Data Wipe

The process of cluster decommissioning encompasses a comprehensive sequence of operations aimed at safely retiring cluster resources while ensuring that residual data artifacts-particularly persistent storage-are rendered irrecoverable. Given the increasing reliance on distributed computing infrastructures for handling sensitive and regulated data, rigor in deprovisioning workflows is paramount to meet both organizational security policies and regulatory frameworks such as GDPR, HIPAA, and PCI-DSS.

A fundamental best practice in cluster decommissioning is to initiate a formal deactivation protocol that prevents new workloads from being scheduled onto the cluster. This is typically achieved by disabling ingress routes and removing the cluster from service registries. This step ensures a quiescent state, diminishing the risk of data inconsistency or loss from in-flight transactions during shutdown. Following operational cessation, administrative access should be leveraged to enumerate all active namespaces, pods, volumes, and associated resources to form a comprehensive inventory of persistent data assets.

Persistent volume claims (PVCs) and the underlying storage volumes attached to a cluster constitute the primary focus for secure data elimination. The choice of data erasure method must be aligned with the sensitivity of the data and the storage medium's characteristics. For magnetic drives, multiple overwrites using standards such as the DoD 5220.22-M method are recommended, whereas solid-state drives require tailored approaches due to wear-leveling mechanisms, often employing cryptographic erasure or device-specific secure erase commands. In cloud-native environments, many cloud providers offer integrated volume snapshot and delete APIs; nevertheless, these operations must be orchestrated with caution, as volume deletions without prior sanitization may not guarantee immediate data unrecoverability.

In Kubernetes-centric architectures, it is advisable to annotate or label persistent volumes with metadata that marks their lifecycle state. Automated scripts or controllers can then target these marked volumes to execute defined data wipe sequences. To provide an example, a data wipe sequence can be implemented in a controlled batch job that mounts the target volume, overwrites the entire data region with pseudorandom bytes, and verifies successful execution prior to volume release:

```
kubectl run wipe-pvc-job --rm -i --tty --image=alpine -- /bin/sh
  -c "
apk add --no-cache dd coreutils &&
mount /dev/sdx /mnt &&
dd if=/dev/urandom of=/mnt/zero.fill bs=1M status=progress &&
sync &&
umount /mnt
"
```

This method ensures that overwrites cover the entire filesystem area, mitigating the risk of data retention remnants. Verification steps involving cryptographic hash comparisons or readback checks may be implemented for enhanced assurance.

Compliance regimes often require auditable proof of data destruction. Automation strategies should therefore generate and centrally store logs capturing the execution timeline, identifiers of erased volumes, operator credentials, and the applied wiping method. Integration with Security Information and Event Management (SIEM) systems provides a robust evidential trail, crucial for audit readiness. Where regulatory mandates prescribe specific retention or destruction schedules, decommissioning plans must incorporate retention period checks and enforce data masking or encryption key destruction prior to physical data deletion, amplifying security with cryptographic controls.

Beyond data erasure, complete decommissioning must address ancillary considerations pertaining to cluster components such as configuration files, certificates, user credentials, and secrets stored within key management systems or vaults. These sensitive materials should undergo secure deletion or key revocation to prevent potential unauthorized resurrection of access privileges. Any backups or snapshots external to the cluster also demand examination to avoid unintended data persistence.

Integration of cluster decommissioning protocols into larger infrastructure-as-code (IaC) pipelines enhances reproducibility and reduces the risk of human error. Declarative manifests can codify resource teardown steps, while specialized operators or controllers embedded into the cluster management platform can enforce compliance at scale. It is critical to perform end-to-end testing of decommissioning flows in non-production environments to evaluate the efficacy of the wipe patterns and adherence to organizational security baselines before executing in live data centers or cloud regions.

In environments managing highly regulated information, the intersection of technical and legal requirements necessitates periodic reassessment of decommissioning procedures. Advances in storage technologies and emerging threat vectors demand evolving best practices, such as implementing hardware encryption on volumes to facilitate rapid cryptographic erasure or incorporating zero-trust principles to minimize residual attack surface post-retirement.

Ultimately, secure cluster decommissioning is a multidisciplinary endeavor requiring coordination between system administrators, security teams, compliance officers, and auditors. Adopting a principled approach that couples rigorous data erasure techniques with comprehensive documentation and automation significantly mitigates risks, fosters regulatory adherence, and upholds organizational trust in the lifecycle management of distributed computing resources.

Chapter 9

Advanced Use Cases and Integration Patterns

K3s isn't just a smaller Kubernetes—it unlocks entirely new possibilities. This chapter goes beyond the basics, exploring how K3s powers next-generation workloads at the edge, infuses AI into constrained environments, and integrates with emerging technologies. Dive into practical blueprints and future-looking strategies to fully unleash the potential of lightweight container orchestration.

9.1. K3s in Edge & IoT Ecosystems

Operating large fleets of K3s clusters in edge and Internet of Things (IoT) environments requires specialized strategies tailored to the unique constraints and requirements of these domains. Unlike traditional centralized data centers, edge and IoT systems consist of geographically dispersed nodes with intermittent connectivity, limited computational resources, and diverse hardware profiles. The lightweight Kubernetes distribution K3s, designed for such environments, enables container orchestration at the edge but necessitates advanced methods for fleet management, data handling, and system resilience.

Fleet Management at Scale

Managing numerous K3s clusters across various edge locations imposes significant operational complexity. To address this, federated or hierarchical control plane architectures are employed, enabling centralized governance while preserving local autonomy. A common approach integrates a central management platform that performs lifecycle operations such as provisioning, scaling, and patching through automated workflows and declarative configurations.

Automation layers built with GitOps principles, often leveraging tools like Flux or Argo CD, provide version-controlled cluster manifests that simplify synchronization and rollback processes. These systems propagate desired state configurations to edge clusters via secure, efficient communication channels, tolerating intermittent connectivity by employing local caching and reconciliation loops within K3s agents.

To optimize bandwidth and reduce overhead, management systems incorporate incremental update mechanisms, transferring only delta changes rather than full manifests or container images. Additionally, change management policies prioritize updates based on cluster criticality, usage patterns, and operational policies, enabling staged rollouts and minimizing disruptions.

Data Aggregation and Event Processing

Edge and IoT deployments generate vast volumes of time-sensitive and heterogeneous data streams, requiring efficient local processing and aggregation to reduce latency and bandwidth consumption. K3s clusters often host distributed data ingestion pipelines and stream processing frameworks, such as lightweight versions of Apache NiFi, Kafka, or custom event-driven microservices, tailored for resource-constrained nodes.

Local data aggregation summarizes sensor readings and telemetry into condensed forms or actionable events, employing time-series databases or in-memory caches optimized for edge environments. This reduces upstream data transmission and facilitates near-real-time decision making.

Event-driven architectures built on Kubernetes primitives, including Custom Resource Definitions (CRDs) and Operators, enable modular and declarative orchestration of data flows. For instance, an Operator might dynamically scale ingress components based on workload intensity or reconfigure processing topology to prioritize critical event streams.

Effective event processing at the edge often involves complex coordination across distributed K3s clusters. Solutions incorporate message brokering and state synchronization protocols designed for unreliable networks, applying conflict-free replicated data types (CRDTs) or event sourcing techniques to maintain consistency without centralized coordination.

Remote Updates and Security Considerations

Remote software and configuration updates are pivotal to maintaining security, functionality, and compliance in dispersed K3s fleets. Secure update pipelines employ mutual TLS authentication, role-based access control, and end-to-end encryption to safeguard communication between management servers and edge clusters.

The ephemeral and sometimes disconnected nature of edge nodes calls for resilient update mechanisms. Atomic update strategies ensure that software upgrades are either fully applied or safely rolled back, preventing partial or inconsistent states. Images and manifests are digitally signed and verified by agents prior to deployment, mitigating supply chain risks.

Update orchestration frameworks incorporate health checks and canary deployments to detect failures early and minimize impact. In scenarios with restricted connectivity, update agents cache necessary binaries and metadata, enabling offline installation and gradual synchronization upon reconnection.

K3s clusters themselves often integrate lightweight certificate authorities and automated renewal tooling (e.g., cert-manager) to manage node identity and encryption certificates autonomously. This facilitates secure communication within and across clusters without requiring constant manual intervention.

Architectural Patterns for Resilience

Designing resilient K3s deployments at the edge and in IoT ecosystems involves embracing failure as an intrinsic property. Clusters are architected for high availability by distributing workloads and state across nodes and regions, limiting the blast radius of individual failures.

Stateless microservices dominate the application landscape, enabling automatic rescheduling and rapid recovery. Stateful workloads, such as databases or caches, rely on replication, leader election protocols, and self-healing Operators to maintain consistency and availability despite network partitions or hardware faults.

Observability is central to resilience. Distributed tracing, metrics aggregation, and log collection are adapted for low-bandwidth links, often employing hierarchical telemetry pipelines where local collectors summarize data before forwarding to central monitoring systems.

Service meshes tailored for edge improve communication reliability and security between distributed services, providing features such as circuit breaking, retry mechanisms, and mutual TLS with minimal resource footprint.

Finally, the intrinsic heterogeneity of edge hardware encourages the use of abstraction layers that encapsulate platform-specific differences. This includes container runtimes optimized for various architectures (ARM, x86) and device plugins exposing specialized hardware capabilities (e.g., GPUs, sensors) to containerized workloads uniformly.

The orchestration of large K3s fleets in edge and IoT settings hinges on reconciling centralized control with decentralized execution, efficient data handling under constrained conditions, robust update mechanisms, and architectural practices designed to embrace and mitigate inevitable failures. These strategies collectively empower organizations to leverage Kubernetes' agility and scalability at the furthest reaches of their digital infrastructure.

9.2. AI/ML Workloads on K3s

K3s, as a lightweight Kubernetes distribution, is specifically designed to meet the constraints of resource-limited environments such as edge and IoT devices. This characteristic positions K3s as a compelling platform for deploying artificial intelligence (AI) and machine learning (ML) workloads in distributed, decentralized scenarios where latency, bandwidth, and operational overhead must be minimized. Deploying AI/ML workloads on K3s requires a nuanced understanding of framework compatibility, resource scheduling challenges, and optimizations tailored to lightweight and heterogeneous hardware architectures.

Framework Compatibility and Containerization

AI/ML workloads typically rely on well-established frameworks such as TensorFlow, PyTorch, ONNX Runtime, and more lightweight inference engines like TensorFlow Lite or OpenVINO for edge inference. These frameworks can be containerized and orchestrated within K3s clusters, enabling seamless scaling and management. However, careful selection of the base images and dependency sets is crucial to ensure that containers remain small enough to conform to edge device storage constraints and to reduce network transfer overhead.

The adoption of multi-arch container images is critical, as edge devices and gateways often utilize ARM or other non-x86 architectures. Tools like Docker Buildx enable building cross-platform images with the necessary AI runtimes preinstalled, facilitating consistent deployment across diverse hardware. For example, TensorFlow Lite models packaged in containers with TensorFlow Lite runtime libraries can be efficiently deployed on ARM64-based K3s nodes without significant compromise in inference speed.

Resource Scheduling and Load Management

K3s's Kubernetes-compatible scheduler, while simplified to maintain a lightweight footprint, supports essential features necessary for effective resource management of AI/ML workloads. Given that ML jobs are typically demanding in terms of CPU, memory, and sometimes GPU/TPU acceleration, resource requests and limits must be precisely declared within pod specifications. This can prevent resource contention and ensure Quality of Service (QoS) for critical workloads.

In edge environments, the scarcity of GPU resources poses a significant scheduling challenge. While K3s supports device plugins to expose hardware accelerators, the heterogeneity of hardware necessitates dynamic scheduling policies sensitive to node capabilities. Labeling nodes with hardware-specific attributes (e.g., `accelerator=arm_ethos` or `gpu=nvidia_t4`) enables affinity-based scheduling, allowing workload pods to be dispatched only on compatible hardware. Furthermore, leveraging Kubernetes taints and tolerations can isolate ML workloads to specific nodes, optimizing resource utilization without disturbing other system functions.

Optimization Strategies for Lightweight and Edge Hardware

AI/ML workloads on resource-constrained environments benefit significantly from model and infrastructure-level optimizations. Model quantization, pruning, and knowledge distillation reduce the computational footprint and memory requirements of neural networks, making them more suitable for edge inference on devices orchestrated by K3s. The deployment process in K3s can be augmented with CI/CD pipelines that automate the conversion and optimization of models before container image build and deployment stages.

From an infrastructure perspective, tuning container runtime parameters such as CPU shares, memory limits, and enabling swap efficiently impact workload stability and responsiveness. Techniques such as lightweight network overlays reduce network stack overhead, while local persistent storage solutions-like hostPath or lightweight distributed file systems (e.g., K3s's built-in Traefik ingress with local PVs)-ensure efficient management of datasets and model artifacts.

Deployment Scenarios: Inferencing and On-Device Learning

Deployed AI/ML workloads on K3s can span a spectrum from inferencing-only tasks to more complex on-device learning (or continual learning). For inferencing, the canonical use case involves deploying trained models as microservices within containers managed by K3s pods. These microservices expose REST or gRPC endpoints, allowing downstream applications or edge sensors to submit real-time data for classification or prediction. The minimal overhead of K3s allows rapid deployment cycles and easy rollbacks or updates, critical for iterative model improvements at the edge.

On-device learning represents a more challenging paradigm, involving incremental training or fine-tuning directly on edge nodes. This usually requires access to local datasets and efficient GPU/TPU utilization to accommodate incremental backpropagation steps. Containerized pipelines can orchestrate this learning process, managing checkpoints and synchronizing updated models back to centralized repositories or federated learning coordinators. K3s's lightweight architecture ensures such workloads impose minimal additional system overhead, thereby extending battery life and maintaining system stability in edge devices.

```
apiVersion: v1
kind: Pod
metadata:
  name: tflite-inference
  labels:
    app: ai-inference
spec:
  nodeSelector:
    kubernetes.io/arch: arm64
  containers:
  - name: tflite-container
    image: myrepo/tflite-runtime:arm64
    resources:
      requests:
        cpu: "500m"
        memory: "256Mi"
      limits:
        cpu: "1"
        memory: "512Mi"
    ports:
    - containerPort: 8080
    command: ["./serve_model"]
    args: ["--model", "/models/mobilenetv2.tflite"]
```

```
$ kubectl get pods
NAME             READY   STATUS    RESTARTS   AGE
tflite-inference 1/1     Running   0          5m
```

Security and Privacy Considerations

AI/ML workloads at the edge often deal with sensitive data. K3s facilitates secure deployment through native Kubernetes mechanisms such as Secrets and ConfigMaps for managing credentials and configurations. Integrating hardware-backed security modules (e.g., TPMs) and leveraging service mesh technologies compatible with K3s (such as lightweight versions of Istio or Linkerd) enhance mutual authentication, encryption, and traffic policy enforcement between AI service components. These security measures are crucial when deploying on-device learning that stores or processes raw data, ensuring compliance with data sovereignty requirements and reducing the risk of data leakage.

K3s's intrinsic design for lightweight operation combined with Kubernetes-native orchestration capabilities offers a versatile foundation for running AI/ML workloads at the edge. Success hinges upon thoughtful container design, efficient resource scheduling respecting device constraints, and deployment paradigms that balance inferencing needs versus incremental learning. By embracing hardware-aware optimization and security best practices, AI/ML deployments can fully leverage K3s's minimalistic platform to deliver impactful intelligence with maximal operational efficiency in edge computing environments.

9.3. Custom Controller and Operator Design

Kubernetes controllers and operators serve as the foundational components for automating the management of resources and extending cluster capabilities to meet domain-specific requirements. Within the lightweight Kubernetes ecosystem of K3s, these constructs must be adapted to accommodate unique operational constraints such as limited resource availability, streamlined security models, and simplified cluster dynamics. The design of custom controllers and operators tailored to K3s environments involves leveraging the Kubernetes control loop pattern while optimizing for footprint, efficiency, and compatibility.

At its core, a Kubernetes controller implements a reconciliation loop that continuously compares the current cluster state against the desired state defined in custom resources and takes corrective actions accordingly. Operators extend this pattern by encapsulating not only the control logic but also domain-specific knowledge, enabling higher-level abstractions for managing complex applications or infrastructure components.

Defining Custom Resource Definitions (CRDs) for Specialized Workloads

Custom Resource Definitions form the schema and API surface for operators to extend Kubernetes with novel resource types. When designing CRDs for K3s, it is critical to minimize the resource schema complexity to reduce API server overhead. For specialized workloads such as IoT edge devices or constrained CI pipelines, CRDs should specify only essential state fields and status attributes, avoiding unnecessary optional fields that complicate reconciliation logic and increase controller processing time.

A practical approach involves performing a domain analysis to enumerate the exact configuration parameters and operational metadata needed. This leads to lean CRDs, which promote faster serialization, lower storage costs in etcd, and reduced network payload sizes during synchronization across lightweight clusters.

Implementing the Reconciliation Loop under K3s Constraints

Custom controllers in K3s must be designed for efficiency and resilience with limited CPU and memory budgets. The canonical reconciliation loop involves fetching resource state, performing validation and business logic, and issuing Kubernetes API calls to converge the observed state towards the desired specification.

To optimize this cycle within K3s:

- Employ client-go caching mechanisms to reduce API calls and improve responsiveness.

- Use event-driven informers to trigger reconciliations only when relevant resource changes occur, minimizing unnecessary wake-ups.

- Implement reconciliation logic idempotently to gracefully handle retries and partial failures, essential in fluctuating edge environments.

- Enforce minimal requeue intervals and exponential backoff strategies to prevent thrashing when dependent resources or external systems are temporarily unavailable.

A representative controller reconcile function skeleton might appear as follows:

```
func (r *CustomResourceReconciler) Reconcile(ctx context.Context,
    req ctrl.Request) (ctrl.Result, error) {
    // Fetch the resource instance
    instance := &customv1alpha1.MyResource{}
    if err := r.Get(ctx, req.NamespacedName, instance); err !=
    nil {
        if apierrors.IsNotFound(err) {
            // Resource deleted, no action needed
            return ctrl.Result{}, nil
        }
        return ctrl.Result{}, err
    }

    // Validate spec fields and adjust status
    if err := validateSpec(instance.Spec); err != nil {
        // Update status to indicate error
        instance.Status.State = "Error"
        instance.Status.Message = err.Error()
        _ = r.Status().Update(ctx, instance)
        return ctrl.Result{}, nil
    }

    // Perform domain-specific reconciliation
    if err := r.handleBusinessLogic(ctx, instance); err != nil {
        return ctrl.Result{RequeueAfter: time.Minute}, err
    }

    // Update status to Ready condition
    instance.Status.State = "Ready"
    _ = r.Status().Update(ctx, instance)

    return ctrl.Result{}, nil
}
```

Operator Patterns Tailored for K3s

Operators deploy a wider spectrum of application lifecycle management, enabling automated installation, configuration, upgrades, backups, and failure recovery. In K3s, operators need to respect constraints such as:

- **Reduced Default RBAC and Security Contexts:** Operators must explicitly request minimal permissions, ensuring compatibility with K3s' lean default roles and avoiding privilege escalation denied by lightweight policies.

- **Single-Node or Air-Gapped Deployments:** Many K3s users operate single-node clusters or environments without external connectivity. Operators should avoid external dependencies at runtime, bundle necessary binaries or container images, and design offline-compatible workflows.

- **Multi-Architecture Support:** K3s is commonly used on ARM-based devices; operators should incorporate multi-architecture manifests and conditional logic for resource creation.

The operator reconciler leverages a modular approach, isolating concerns such as CRD validation, dependency creation (e.g., ConfigMaps, Secrets), and reconciliation of external systems to maintain clarity and enable selective invocation. Employing custom predicates and controller-runtime options can further tune event filtering to prevent unnecessary reconciliations in resource-constrained settings.

Integration with K3s-Specific Features and Constraints

Distinctive K3s components such as the embedded SQLite datastore or external database options influence controller and operator design decisions. When operating with embedded SQLite, controllers should reduce the volume and frequency of API writes and finalizer updates to mitigate bottlenecks. Persistent watchers and excessive status updates can degrade performance; thus, careful batching and aggregation of status fields are recommended.

K3s also integrates Traefik ingress and lightweight service mesh options; operators managing networking resources need to conform to these predefined configurations and avoid assumptions valid only for standard Kubernetes distributions.

Testing and Validation Under K3s

Effective development must incorporate testing strategies that simulate K3s cluster behavior. Using K3s-in-Docker or K3d toolings facilitates realistic API behavior and version compatibility validation. Unit tests should mock Kubernetes client interfaces for isolated logic validation, while end-to-end tests deploy operators onto ephemeral K3s clusters to assess real reconciliation cycles, resource usage, and failure handling.

Continuous integration pipelines tailored for multi-architecture builds and lightweight images ensure operator artifacts remain consistent with K3s resource limitations. Metrics and logs from operators should be instrumented with lightweight exporters compatible with K3s telemetry stack or external observability tools.

Summary of Best Practices

- Design CRDs with minimal and precise schema definitions to reduce processing overhead.

- Implement idempotent, event-driven reconciliation loops optimized with local caching and backoff strategies.

- Ensure RBAC manifests align precisely with K3s default permissions and avoid unnecessary privileges.

- Incorporate offline and multi-architecture support for robustness across K3s deployment scenarios.

- Batch status updates and limit API interactions to prevent SQLite performance degradation in single-node clusters.

- Utilize K3s-specific tooling in testing to replicate cluster constraints and validate operator behavior comprehensively.

Through careful attention to these patterns and constraints, custom controllers and operators can effectively extend K3s clusters in specialized domains, enabling automation and operational excellence without sacrificing the lightweight and resource-efficient nature of the platform.

9.4. Hybrid Cloud and On-Prem Orchestration

Orchestrating K3s clusters across hybrid cloud and on-premises infrastructures involves designing an architecture that balances connectivity, policy enforcement, resilience, and seamless integration between heterogeneous environments. Given the lightweight nature of K3s, it is particularly well-suited to distributed environments with resource-constrained edge nodes. However, its orchestration across multi-tenant and geographically dispersed infrastructures introduces distinct challenges and best practices that require careful consideration.

A foundational architectural principle is to establish a unified control plane or a federated control architecture that can manage disparate K3s clusters while respecting domain and tenancy boundaries. A common approach is to deploy a centralized management plane-often hosted in a secure cloud environment-that maintains cluster state, orchestrates upgrades, and enforces policies centrally. Direct control plane exposure between cloud and on-prem clusters is generally avoided due to latency, security, and connectivity constraints. Instead, lightweight agents installed within each K3s cluster handle localized decisions and policy enforcement, syncing asynchronously with the central management plane.

Connectivity paradigms for hybrid orchestration frequently employ VPNs, SD-WAN overlays, or service mesh technologies to enable secure, reliable communication channels. For example, integrating WireGuard VPN tunnels or leveraging cloud provider private link capabilities can ensure encrypted, low-latency paths between control endpoints and worker nodes spread across data centers and cloud regions. Service meshes such as Istio or Linkerd, compatible with K3s deployments, provide additional capabilities like mutual TLS, traffic shaping, and observability across cluster boundaries, simplifying microservice communication and secure ingress/egress routing.

Policy enforcement in hybrid and multi-tenant scenarios requires fine-grained, declarative frameworks that maintain consistency without compromising flexibility. Tools like Open Policy Agent (OPA) Gatekeeper or Kyverno can be embedded in each K3s cluster to enforce security, resource quotas, and compliance standards locally, while centralized policy repositories propagate updates uniformly. Role-Based Access Control (RBAC) and network policies must be designed to partition tenant namespaces strictly, preventing cross-tenant resource access and data leakage. Applying admission controllers at the cluster ingress points enforces these policies early in the deployment pipeline, reducing attack surfaces.

Failover and disaster recovery strategies are crucial in hybrid cloud orchestration to maintain application availability despite regional outages or network partitions. K3s enables lightweight cluster federation approaches, where applications replicate state across clusters using tools like Velero for backup and restore, or multi-cluster service meshes for traffic failover. It is common to configure active-active or active-passive models: for example, an on-prem K3s cluster may serve primary workloads with cloud-based clusters standing by to absorb traffic if the primary becomes unavailable. Stateful applications require consistent data replication, achievable via distributed databases or leveraging cloud-native storage replication mechanisms integrated through Kubernetes persistent volume abstractions.

Integration points between on-premises environments and cloud platforms frequently include CI/CD pipelines, logging and monitoring stacks, and centralized identity providers. CI/CD tools, such as Jenkins or GitLab CI, must be capable of deploying seamlessly into multiple K3s clusters without manual intervention. Leveraging Kubernetes-native package managers like Helm or Flux can automate the promotion and synchronization of application manifests across clusters. For observability, aggregating telemetry data from diverse environments into a unified dashboard-using Prometheus federation or centralized logging pipelines with Elasticsearch, Fluentd, and Kibana (EFK)-facilitates rapid incident detection and root cause analysis. Authentication and authorization systems should integrate with enterprise identity solutions via OpenID Connect or LDAP, providing seamless single sign-on and consistent access controls across all cluster environments.

Special attention must be paid to network address translation, DNS resolution, and service discovery across hybrid domains. Cross-cluster DNS forwarding or global service registries help applications resolve endpoints irrespective of their hosting location, while network policies and firewalls must be aligned to permit legitimate cross-site traffic while limiting potential attack vectors. The deployment of ingress controllers at each boundary-configured for secure TLS termination and routing-ensures controlled ingress of external requests and enables load balancing across clusters.

Another key consideration is the automation of cluster lifecycle management, including provisioning, scaling, patching, and upgrade workflows. Tools like Cluster API, combined with infrastructure-as-code frameworks (Terraform, Ansible), provide declarative mechanisms to standardize cluster creation and maintain consistent configurations-even across disparate infrastructure providers. In multi-tenant setups, namespaces and resource quotas must be scoped dynamically to prevent resource contention, while monitoring policies ensure proactive capacity planning and anomaly detection.

Hybrid cloud and on-prem orchestration of K3s clusters demands a coherent strategy that integrates secure connectivity, robust policy enforcement, resilient failover mechanisms, and unified observability. Deploying federated or centralized control planes augmented by local agents strikes a balance between consistency and autonomy. Carefully engineered network fabrics, automated lifecycle management, and aligned security frameworks enable mixed environments to operate as a cohesive platform, empowering organizations to leverage the agility of cloud resources alongside the control of on-premises infrastructure.

9.5. Legacy Application Modernization with K3s

Modernizing legacy applications for deployment on lightweight Kubernetes distributions such as K3s requires a comprehensive approach addressing both architectural and operational paradigms unique to containerized environments. Legacy systems often exhibit monolithic structures with stateful components, so migrating them to cloud-native platforms demands careful planning around data management, service decomposition, and incremental adaptation to minimize disruption.

The initial step in migrating legacy applications to K3s involves a thorough assessment of the existing application architecture. This includes identifying tightly coupled modules, stateful components such as databases or session stores, and interfaces that interact with external services. A critical objective is establishing a target architecture that leverages K3s' lightweight Kubernetes control plane while ensuring operational efficiency on resource-constrained environments.

A practical blueprint begins with containerizing the application. For monolithic legacy applications, this often entails packaging the entire application into a single Docker container. However, this strategy, while straightforward, limits scalability and fails to exploit Kubernetes-native resilience patterns. Therefore, it is essential to consider refactoring or componentization concurrent with containerization, enabling the gradual transition toward microservices or modular architectures.

Data management poses a significant challenge in migrating stateful legacy applications. K3s' support for persistent volumes enables flexible storage solutions but requires explicit configuration to ensure data integrity and availability.

Two primary data migration approaches are recommended:

1. **Lift-and-Shift with Persistent Volumes:** This involves moving the existing database or stateful data stores as-is into persistent volumes managed by K3s. For example, using `hostPath` volumes for small-scale clusters or integrating with network-attached storage backends compatible with Kubernetes. This approach maintains the legacy database unchanged while benefiting from container orchestration.

2. **Incremental Data Refactoring and Synchronization:** The data layer is incrementally migrated to cloud-native databases or managed database services that Kubernetes applications can seamlessly access. Synchronization mechanisms ensure data consistency between legacy and new systems during the migration window. This technique supports ongoing operation with minimal downtime.

A critical configuration element in this context is the use of `StatefulSets` for deploying stateful applications on K3s. `StatefulSets` guarantee stable network identities and persistent storage, critical for legacy applications migrating to container orchestration.

Refactoring workflows to adapt to Kubernetes' operational model is essential for performance, scalability, and maintainability.

Legacy applications often rely on vertical scaling and assume a static runtime environment, incompatible with Kubernetes' horizontal scaling and dynamic scheduling.

Key refactoring strategies include:

- *Breaking down monoliths*: Decompose monolithic applications into modular components deployable as independent microservices. This decomposition enhances scalability and facilitates deployment on multiple nodes within a K3s cluster.

- *Designing stateless services*: Rework application logic to externalize session state and avoid local storage dependency. Shared caches or distributed databases can maintain state externally, enabling easier scaling and failover.

- *Implementing health checks and readiness probes*: Integrate Kubernetes-native liveness and readiness probes to allow the orchestrator to monitor application health and manage container lifecycle effectively.

- *Utilizing ConfigMaps and Secrets*: Externalize configuration from application images using ConfigMaps and Secrets, fostering environment agnosticism and promoting secure handling of sensitive data.

To mitigate risks associated with wholesale rewrites, incremental modernization offers a pragmatic pathway. This strategy involves progressively migrating individual components of a legacy application to microservices running on K3s, while other parts continue operation in the existing environment. Common techniques include:

- **Strangler Pattern**: Encapsulate legacy functionality behind new service APIs deployed in K3s. Over time, redirect traffic from legacy modules to containerized services, eventually phasing out legacy components.

- **Sidecar Containers**: Inject proxy or adapter containers alongside legacy applications to provide standardized logging, monitoring, or networking capabilities without modifying core application code.

- **Facade Services**: Implement lightweight facade services that abstract legacy interfaces and translate them to modern protocols or APIs consumable by new K3s workloads.

- **Blue-Green Deployment**: Exploit Kubernetes' rolling update capabilities to deploy modernized services alongside existing ones, switching traffic incrementally to minimize downtime and validate performance.

This incremental approach allows teams to harness the benefits of Kubernetes orchestration on K3s without necessitating immediate, comprehensive rewrites.

Operating legacy applications within a K3s cluster also demands attention to cluster resource constraints and simplifications characteristic of K3s deployments. Given K3s' design for edge and resource-limited environments, memory and CPU overheads must be scrutinized during migration. Lightweight application profiles and minimalist base images improve compatibility with K3s' low resource footprint.

Integration with Kubernetes-native logging and monitoring, such as Fluentd, Prometheus, and Grafana running with minimal configurations, ensures observability essential for legacy application management. Defining resource requests and limits explicitly prevents unexpected evictions and ensures stable cluster operation.

Finally, robust CI/CD pipelines enable automated builds, tests, and deployments targeting K3s clusters, facilitating rapid iteration and reducing operational risk during modernization.

```
apiVersion: apps/v1
kind: StatefulSet
metadata:
  name: legacy-db
spec:
  serviceName: "legacy-db-service"
  replicas: 1
  selector:
    matchLabels:
      app: legacy-db
  template:
    metadata:
      labels:
        app: legacy-db
    spec:
      containers:
      - name: legacy-db-container
        image: legacy-db-image:latest
        ports:
        - containerPort: 5432
        volumeMounts:
        - name: db-data
          mountPath: /var/lib/postgresql/data
  volumeClaimTemplates:
  - metadata:
      name: db-data
    spec:
      accessModes: [ "ReadWriteOnce" ]
      resources:
        requests:
          storage: 10Gi
```

```
NAME          READY   STATUS    RESTARTS   AGE
legacy-db-0   1/1     Running   0          48h
```

By combining structured refactoring strategies with Kubernetes-native resource management and deployment blueprints, legacy applications can be effectively modernized to run on K3s clusters. Such modernization enhances operational agility, resource efficiency, and sets the foundation for ongoing evolution within cloud-native ecosystems.

9.6. Extending K3s with WASM and Non-Container Workloads

The evolution of Kubernetes distributions such as K3s has increasingly embraced lightweight and flexible workload models beyond traditional containerized applications. Among these, WebAssembly (WASM) and other non-containerized workloads present a compelling opportunity to expand the operational surface while maintaining the core principles of Kubernetes orchestration. This section explores the architectural integration of WASM runtimes into K3s, design considerations for non-container workload execution, and effective best practices to adopt these emerging paradigms.

K3s's architecture, optimized for resource-constrained environments, provides an ideal foundation to incorporate WebAssembly workloads. WASM, originally devised for high-performance browser applications, now supports server-side use cases with runtimes such as Wasmtime, Wasmer, and WasmEdge. Unlike containers, WASM modules are sandboxed bytecode binaries offering instantaneous start-up, fine-grained resource isolation, and deterministic performance characteristics.

Integrating WASM into K3s requires incorporating a WASM runtime as a first-class citizen alongside container runtimes like containerd. There are primarily two architectural approaches:

- *Sidecar or Embedded Runtime*: Embedding the WASM runtime into the container runtime layer or as a dedicated sidecar container allows coexistence with container workloads while isolating WASM execution environments. This preserves the standard Kubernetes pod abstraction but invokes the WASM runtime for specific workloads.

- *Native Runtime Integration*: Developing custom Kubernetes runtime classes or using runtime extensions (via

246

the Container Runtime Interface extended mechanisms) to directly schedule WASM modules without traditional container images, thereby removing the container dependency altogether.

In K3s, the lightweight nature and extensibility simplify runtime integration, as the overall footprint overhead of deploying WASM environments is significantly reduced compared to heavier Kubernetes distributions. Moreover, the distribution's in-built manifest controllers and CRD (Custom Resource Definitions) patterns facilitate defining dedicated resource types for WASM workloads.

A critical element of running WASM in K3s is the runtime orchestration stack. The commonly adopted implementation includes:

- **WASM Runtime Selection**: WasmEdge is notable for cloud-native applications due to its system interface support (WASI), low latency, and multi-language bindings, making it suitable for edge and IoT scenarios that K3s often targets.

- **Kubernetes Custom Resources**: Defining `WasmWorkload` or equivalent CRDs to encapsulate WASM module metadata, runtime parameters, and resource limits. This declarative approach aligns with Kubernetes principles and enables native API interaction.

- **Operator or Controller**: Implementing a controller that reconciles the lifecycle of WASM workloads, ensuring deployment to nodes with compatible runtime environments, health monitoring, and failure recovery.

- **Scheduling Policies**: Extending the Kubernetes scheduler or using node affinity and taints/tolerations to schedule WASM workloads to nodes with the requisite runtime capabilities, thus isolating them from nodes running traditional containers or other workload types.

The interaction between the WASM runtime and containerized components may involve network proxies or API gateways to facilitate communication. Service meshes and ingress controllers can be extended to support WASM-based microservices, thereby achieving seamless interoperability within K3s clusters.

The paradigm shift toward non-container workloads requires deliberate operational strategies:

- **Design for Portability and Security**: WASM modules, due to their sandboxed nature, reduce attack surfaces; nevertheless, strict runtime-security policies should be enforced, using Kubernetes RBAC (Role Based Access Control) and network policies to contain possible vulnerabilities.

- **Resource Management**: Unlike containers with cgroup-based resource isolation, WASM runtimes rely on alternative sandboxing mechanisms. Employ resource quotas and limits with awareness of runtime constraints, such as memory linearity and CPU utilization limits supported by the WASM engine.

- **Observability and Telemetry**: Integrate monitoring at the runtime level using Prometheus exporters and tracing frameworks that support WASM environments. Identifying runtime metrics and error conditions early aids in diagnosing issues unique to non-container workloads.

- **Lifecycle Management**: Utilize declarative infrastructure as code practices to manage WASM deployments, leveraging Helm charts or Kustomize overlays enhanced with WASM-specific parameters.

- **Hybrid Workload Orchestration**: Exploit K3s's flexibility to co-deploy containers and WASM modules, using workload scheduling policies to optimize node resource utilization and meet latency or throughput objectives.

- **Incremental Migration Strategies**: For existing containerized applications, consider breaking down monolithic services into smaller WASM modules for performance-critical or edge-executed functions while retaining containers for complex or stateful components.

In addition to WebAssembly, other emerging non-container workload formats are compatible with K3s's modularity:

- **Unikernels**: Specialized single-application kernels provide minimal overhead and high security. K3s can schedule unikernel images through runtime adaptations, requiring custom runtime integration like Kata Containers or Firecracker.

- **MicroVMs**: Lightweight virtual machines that blend VM isolation with rapid start-up credentials are scheduled alongside container workloads, handled via CRI-compatible runtimes.

- **Function-as-a-Service (FaaS) Models**: Serverless paradigms using WASM or tiny execution units allow event-driven scaling on K3s, enabled by function controllers that interface with the Kubernetes API.

- **IoT and Edge Native Workloads**: Non-container workloads designed for constrained devices leverage K3s's tailored footprint, using direct binary deployments or embedded runtime modules managed via Kubernetes abstractions.

The common thread in these patterns is enhanced agility and reduced resource consumption, attributes that complement K3s's lightweight distribution goals. Expanding beyond the traditional container model aligns Kubernetes ecosystems with modern, heterogeneous computing environments.

While WASM and other non-containerized workloads introduce compelling benefits, challenges in debugging, tooling maturity, and ecosystem standardization remain. Achieving seamless runtime interoperability across multiple architectures, enhanced security auditing, and comprehensive lifecycle tooling are topics of ongoing research and development. K3s's modular and extensible architecture positions it advantageously to adapt as these workloads mature, fostering an environment where hybrid Kubernetes clusters can orchestrate diverse execution formats with unified control.

Through thoughtful architectural choices, runtime integration practices, and operational rigor, extending K3s with WASM and non-container workloads unlocks new dimensions of performance, scalability, and flexibility indispensable to next-generation cloud-native applications.

9.7. Future Directions and Roadmap

The K3s project continues to evolve rapidly as a lightweight, fully compliant Kubernetes distribution tailored for edge computing, IoT, and resource-constrained environments. Forecasting its development trajectory involves an intricate understanding of the interplay between emerging technological demands, community-driven enhancements, and inherent architectural constraints. The roadmap ahead is shaped by anticipated feature expansions, increasing community engagement, and persistent operational challenges, each critical to maintaining K3s's relevance and robustness in heterogeneous deployments.

- **Anticipated Feature Enhancements**

    A key focus of future K3s releases involves deepening support for multi-architecture environments. With the proliferation of ARM-based processors and specialized hardware accelerators at the edge, K3s aims to streamline native compatibility and provide optimized binaries that reduce overhead without compromising functionality. Extensions to the built-in container runtime, containerd, are expected to improve container lifecycle management, particularly for low-latency and intermittent connectivity scenarios common in the field.

Another major advancement lies in enhanced security posture through integrated service meshes and improved policy enforcement. K3s plans to incorporate more extensive support for SPIFFE (Secure Production Identity Framework For Everyone) and SPIRE (SPIFFE Runtime Environment) to facilitate workload identity management, ensuring zero-trust principles across distributed node clusters. Additionally, credential and secret management will be refined with tighter integration of external vault solutions, enabling secure and automated secrets provisioning aligned with dynamic operational contexts.

Scalability is receiving renewed attention, with particular emphasis on federated K3s clusters. This work anticipates scenarios requiring thousands of lightweight clusters to operate and coordinate seamlessly across disparate geographical locations. The roadmap includes mechanisms for easier cluster federation, consistent configuration distribution, and optimized cross-cluster networking to support complex multitenant and multi-operator scenarios.

- **Community Initiatives and Ecosystem Growth**

  The strength of the K3s project is inherently tied to its open-source community. The forthcoming period targets expansive community initiatives designed to accelerate adoption and collaborative innovation. A structured program for certification and training of operators and developers is under development, aimed at standardizing expertise levels and encouraging best practices in K3s deployment and management.

  Contribution pathways will be formalized to lower the barrier for newcomers and facilitate focused engagement on emerging subdomains, such as edge AI workloads, data synchronization across constrained links, and event-driven compute patterns native to edge environments. This is complemented by an augmented advisory board comprising stakeholders from cloud providers, hardware manufacturers, and open-source foundations, steering strategic priorities in alignment with broader cloud-native trends.

Efforts to foster a vibrant plugin and extension ecosystem are also a critical roadmap component. By providing standardized APIs and SDKs, K3s is enabling third-party developers to create interoperable network plugins, observability tools, and lifecycle operators that integrate seamlessly at minimal resource expense. Such extensibility ensures that diverse use cases-from industrial automation to smart retail-can tailor the core platform to their specific operational constraints without fragmenting the upstream project.

- **Ongoing Challenges**

Despite the positive outlook, several enduring challenges require careful navigation. First, balancing the minimalism of K3s against the increasing complexity of Kubernetes APIs and ecosystem services remains a nuanced engineering endeavor. Implementing feature parity while preserving a lightweight footprint demands continuous innovation in modular architecture and dependency management.

Network management in edge environments continues to pose issues related to intermittent connectivity, NAT traversal, and dynamic IP addressing. Building resilient communication layers that can gracefully degrade and recover in the face of such network volatility is a nontrivial task, especially when synchronous, cluster-wide consensus protocols are involved.

Another pressing concern is telemetry and observability. Resource scarcity at the edge constrains the deployment of traditional monitoring stacks, yet maintaining operational visibility is vital for fault detection and predictive maintenance. Advancing lightweight yet expressive telemetry standards and aggregators is essential to closing this gap without imposing undue performance penalties.

Finally, as K3s scales across numerous small clusters, sophisticated lifecycle management tools for upgrades, configuration drift detection, and incident response will become indispensable. Developing automated, policy-driven frameworks that can operate under diverse administrative domains is both a technical and organizational challenge that the roadmap addresses incrementally.

- **Engagement Strategies for Operators and Developers**

  Proactive involvement in the K3s development ecosystem enables operators and developers to anticipate changes and contribute effectively. Monitoring the project's GitHub repository and participating in design discussions via mailing lists and community meetings provide early insights into proposed features, deprecations, and architectural shifts. Contributing code, documentation, or test cases directly influences the quality and direction of critical components.

  Integrating K3s into real-world testbeds and sharing use case findings accelerates maturity of features and surfaces edge-specific issues that may otherwise remain latent. Collaborative benchmarking efforts yield metrics that guide optimization priorities and facilitate informed decision-making for deployment architectures.

  Furthermore, contributing plugins, custom resource definitions (CRDs), and automation scripts fosters a collective knowledge base and tooling ecosystem that benefits all stakeholders. Engaging in certification programs and peer training not only elevates personal proficiency but also cultivates a resilient community that can collectively tackle future disruptions and innovations.

In summary, the future trajectory of K3s entails a harmonious synthesis of advancing technical capabilities, broadening community involvement, and overcoming infrastructural challenges peculiar to the edge. This evolving landscape demands that operators and developers remain agile, informed, and proactive to help shape and sustain the platform's continued success.

www.ingramcontent.com/pod-product-compliance
Lightning Source LLC
Chambersburg PA
CBHW061242220326
41599CB00028B/5505